How Not To Build A Pond

From Disaster to Success

by
Susan Trott

Dedication

To all those who long for living water near their home—who may not have the budget, but do have the brawn—this is our story.

Fraught with errors, terrors, and wins, it shows how we built our ponds, what mistakes we made, and how you can avoid them. And if you don't, that's okay. Everything can be fixed.

Above all, remember: to keep a living thing, we must strive to work with Nature, not against Her.

Acknowledgments

Every pond is built with more than stone and water. It's built with hands, hearts, and patience.

First, to my husband Jim—my partner through every disaster, rebuild, and midnight crisis. You hauled rocks, fixed leaks, laughed when we should have cried, and never once said "enough." This book is as much yours as it is mine.

To Eric, our carpenter, with nerves of steel, who never blinked when asked to reinforce basement ponds or clad block walls with cedar.

To Joe, our plumber, who turned pipe and fittings into an art form, and who understood the joy of designing something "unconventional." And to the electricians, landscapers, and countless tradespeople who humored us and made the impossible possible.

To our friends, who helped when they could and reminded me that water is meant to be played in, not just worried over.

And finally, to everyone who dreams of living water in their own backyard—whether you build with shoestring budgets or grand designs—this book is for you. May you learn from our mistakes, laugh at our chaos, and find joy in your own pond journeys.

Why I Solve Things the Way I Do

I don't usually think of myself as a "problem solver."

It's more that I see how things fit together—like gears in a hidden machine.

When something goes wrong, my mind doesn't stop at the symptom.

It starts pulling invisible threads, tracing causes backward and connections sideways.

Very often, by the time someone finishes explaining a problem, I've already spotted the shape of it—and the place where it will come undone.

It's not magic.

It's just how my brain works: finding patterns, mapping systems, and trusting the quiet moment when all the pieces click into place.

That way of thinking is how this pond came to be.

One puzzle at a time.

Susan Trott

Copyright

Table of Contents

How Hard Can It Be?

It was 1998, and we had just bought our first house. I was hooked on the TV show Trading Spaces, which gave me the brilliant idea: I needed a pond. Not a big pond—just something with moving water, a quiet, serene place where I could sit in the morning with my coffee and contemplate nothing.

My "research" lasted about three hours. How hard could it be? Dig a hole, drop in a liner, fill it with water—boom, pond.

By Friday afternoon, I was out in the yard sketching what I proudly called my "Finger Lake in miniature." At its longest it was maybe 15 feet long and 4 feet across, 20 inches deep, both ends pointed. I dug for a day and a half, tossing the soil into a pile with plans to sculpt it into a waterfall.

By Sunday afternoon, the pond was done. That morning we picked up water plants and a handful of 20-cent feeder goldfish. We also got dechlorinator because our municipal water has chloramine in it. That is deadly to fish, so it needed to be neutralized before adding fish.

Our very first pond—a humble "Finger Lake." I thought I was done.

That afternoon my brother showed up. He looked at the pond and said, "Nice. But it needs fish."

1 - *Pretty Pond in Winter*

I told him there were fish—little goldfish. He rolled his eyes and disappeared. Two hours later he returned with a bag. Inside was an adorable six-inch blue fish whiskered 'catfish'.

My husband and I thought he was adorable. We floated the bag, released him into the pond, and named him Caesar.

The next day we went back to the store where and we learned that Caesar was a koi and came home with four more.

15

Koi, we soon discovered, are not catfish or goldfish. They grow large, live for decades, and do not politely stay in tiny ponds.

By fall, our five koi were nearly a foot long. Ottawa winters are long and brutal. There was no way they could stay outside.

So we improvised. We bought preformed pond liners and set them up in the basement with sandbags, patio stones, and grow lights. For the next seven months, our koi lived downstairs.

One thing became very clear that first winter: those fish pooped up a storm. Within weeks, the bottom of that little pond liner was buried in detritus — an unholy carpet of fish poop, leaves, and mystery gunk.

2 - Siphon Vacuuming

I went back to the aquarium store in desperation, hoping for some sage advice. Their solution was a siphon vacuum, so we dutifully returned home armed with that, a test kit, extra dechlorinator, and a small filter.

Siphon vacuuming a pond, I quickly discovered, is not fun. It meant kneeling on cold floor, hunched over the water, painstakingly aiming the siphon at tiny piles of muck while trying not to splash myself in the face. This was nothing like vacuuming a bedroom—it was slow, awkward, and half the time the sludge just swirled around instead of being sucked up.

Oh, how I wished for a better way! The filter we installed did help a little by keeping the water clearer, and the staff also taught us about testing the water—something we hadn't even thought of. That's when I learned the water was far from "healthy," and suddenly we were juggling pH, ammonia, nitrite, nitrate, hardness… and buying little bottles of potions to "balance" it all.

This was way more complicated than the 75-gallon aquarium I'd had years ago.

I needed to learn a whole lot more!

Water changes were an adventure. We siphoned with a garden hose across the basement to the furnace drain, then turned the hose around to fill it again. Inefficient, messy, but it worked.

By the second summer, the koi had doubled in size and appetite. We discovered koi cookies—Cheetos-like puff treats they snatched from our fingers—and watermelon. They weren't keen until I cut a hole in the center of the slice. Then they fought over it. They learned to recognize our voices, following us around the pond like puppies.

> LESSON: The smaller the body of water, the harder it
>   is to keep it balanced.

That second winter indoors, it was clear: they were too big. We needed a bigger pond. I started reading everything I could, and met Gavin—a Navy officer and koi enthusiast who taught me about bacteria, filters, microscopes, and why water chemistry mattered more than fish food.

> LESSON: *You aren't keeping fish—you're keeping water. The fish just live in it.*

Plants help, but they are not efficient enough to do the bacteria's job. To match a good bio-filter, you'd need to plant the entire surface of the pond densely and let it mature for years.

> LESSON: *Plants are not filters. They're helpers.*

Meanwhile, algae throws another curveball. By day it acts like a plant—consuming carbon dioxide and releasing oxygen. By night it flips, consuming oxygen and releasing carbon dioxide. That's why ponds without circulation or filtration often suffocate fish at night, even when they look fine during the day.

And then there's the simple fact: in nature, koi are river fish. They never live in the same water for long, because the current constantly carries waste away. In a backyard pond, the water just sits there unless you intervene.

> LESSON: *Water changes are essential. They simulate the river. Fish should not live in the same water molecules forever.*

When we moved to a new house, I had a plan: a proper koi pond, ten feet across, six feet deep. I hired a contractor who promised he "knew ponds."

3 - 25 ft x 25 ft x 8 ft!

He did not.

A few days before we took possession, a backhoe arrived. We'd marked out a neat circle on the ground. My daughter even drew fish in spray paint. On move-in day, she ran ahead and when we heard her scream, we came running around the corner to find—not a pond—but a 25-by-25-foot hole, eight feet deep.

The only amusing part of the whole ordeal came when we discovered empty beer bottles at the bottom of the big pit. One wall had caved in a bit, and there were clear boot prints pressed into the clay. Apparently, a group of adventurous teenagers had decided our new house was the perfect place to sneak into, party, and make mischief. Instead, they fell into our trap.

Oh, how I would have loved to see their faces when they realized where they'd landed!

Strangely enough, even though break-ins were a known problem in our neighborhood, we never had a single incident again after that.

The contractor didn't seem to realize what the backhoe operator had actually done—a cavernous pit. Instead of rethinking the design, he decided to "make it smaller" by dumping an astonishing thirty tonnes of sand and a full tonne of stone into the hole. Just like that, the pit was half-buried under mountains of fill.

Because the pit was still too wide for the piece of EPDM he had ordered, he "solved" the problem by gluing together scraps of liner to make one big piece. It was a patchwork quilt of black rubber, seams and all.

And somehow, in all of this, he forgot the bottom drains entirely.

The contractor managed to get his liner in the hold by the end of September, which was good, because the fish, who were currently refugees in a tiny tank in our garage, needed somewhere to go. The two-thirds filled "Frankenpond" was deep enough for them we hoped.

Then came Thanksgiving. We returned from a weekend away to find the pond empty, liner collapsed, and the koi half-buried in black water and sand.

That night my husband pulled off a massive rescue of all the fish. While I was setting up that tiny tank in the basement, he was donning three pairs of jeans, hip waders, and two sweatshirts. My husband bravely waded into the near-freezing slurry around midnight to start pulling fish out of the water. Our neighbor Dave took pity on him, and came and helped from the edge, ferrying fish in Rubbermaid tubs. The two of them worked until dawn, rescuing every fish. Only one goldfish was lost. But my poor husband? He ended up sick with double pneumonia for two weeks. But the koi lived.

> LESSON: Always cover new tanks. Fish are escape
> artists; in a panic they will jump.

Back in the basement, the preformed tanks were hopelessly small. They couldn't stay there all winter. So, inspired by my son's Lego blocks, I chalked out a plan and started stacking concrete blocks on the basement floor.

Planning with Lego bricks—scaling up playtime to pond size.

Within a week, we had built a rectangular tank with those blocks and added a liner. It looked good held—until we started to fill it with water. As soon as there was enough water (6-8") we started transferring the fish from their small tank into the new tank. They were clearly grateful to be in something with space again. We watched them swim happily in 8" of water.

As the water reached the top of the second row of blocks, the walls started to bulge outward ever so slightly. By the middle of the third row, our "indoor pond" was becoming a canoe.

> *LESSON:* *Water is heavy. You need solid walls to*
> *hold it back.*

Clearly, this couldn't stay, so we had to react to yet another emergency.

"We can't put the fish back in those small tanks!"

"So we'll fix it with them inside this one."

"How?"

We started draining the tank, with the hose siphoning off the water down the bathroom rough-in in the floor. It was because of that pipe, we could put a pond in the basement. Once the water was down to the top of the first row of bricks, we could straighten the remaining rows above. However, we could not move the bottom row back into line because of the water. We got it close, but not perfect. There was still a curve to the long walls.

The question was: would filling the blocks with cement and rebar be enough?

You should have seen us, carefully rolling back the liner onto a broom handle and pouring cement down the holes one trowel at a time and inserting a piece of rebar, all while the fish were swimming happily around, blissfully unaware of the urgency and disaster they were on the brink of.

I'll say this again, but our fish survived and thrived in spite of us. They were starting to demonstrate one of those qualities the Japanese prize them for: luck.

4 - *Concrete block tank*

19

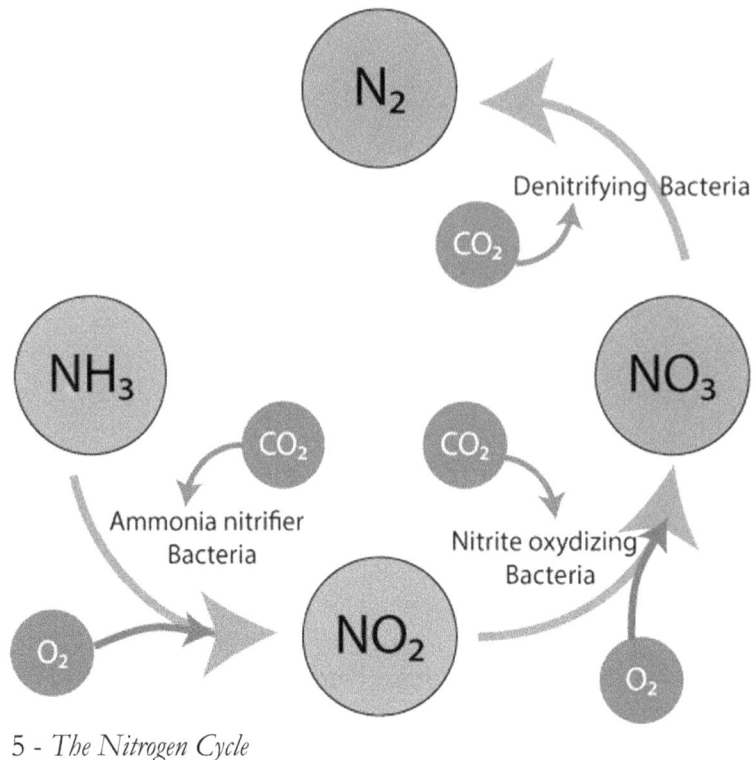

5 - *The Nitrogen Cycle*

The Science: The Nitrogen Cycle

Fish constantly release ammonia (NH3) into the water through respiration and waste. It's poisonous to them.

Bacteria quickly colonize and convert ammonia into nitrite (NO2)—also poisonous.

Thankfully, another bacteria converts nitrite into nitrate (NO3), which is mostly harmless and actually great food for plants.

So water runs in cycles: ammonia → nitrite → nitrate. This is why a pond can stabilize if it has the right bacterial colony.

After the Catastrophe

Dealing with the urgency of the fish, left us exhausted, stressed, and broke. That was an added expense we hadn't been anticipated. We didn't get a chance to really look at what was left of the mess outside for a couple of days. When we did, we stood there and cried.

Where a pond had been, there was nothing but ruin. The liner, the underlayment, the gravel—swallowed by collapsing walls of sand. The hole yawned back at us like an open wound: still roughly 25 feet long, 25 feet wide, and now seven feet deep, filled with loose sand and broken promises. And the contractor? Gone—along with that $4,000. We never saw him again.

In the meantime, we had a new house to set up, boxes to unpack, and kids to get to school. We'd only been here six weeks—how could things have gone so wrong so quickly?

It was already almost Halloween and there was no way to start over before winter. So we turned our backs on that crater and turned our attention to the rest of our life.

6 - Day after the collapse

The Basement Refuge

Our koi were happy in their hastily built basement concrete tank. It had a west-facing window that poured in afternoon light; the koi would drift there like cats to a sunny square. Koi and cats share that in common: they love the sun.

The setup was crude: no bottom drain, no skimmer, and a Frankenfilter cobbled together from whatever free samples we could wrangle (my husband was writing for Koi World then; advertisers sent pumps and filters to test—some worked, many didn't).

LESSON: *Always use equipment sized correctly for your pond.*

21

The basement tank was nearly 2,000 gallons with six or seven koi and about twenty goldfish (of course they bred). It needed at least one full turnover per hour; we were lucky to manage half that.

Improvisation kept us afloat. We hit a local recycler called Cohen's (they recycle materials from old buildings that are to be torn down) and found old food-grade olive barrels for $15 apiece, and a huge roll of nylon strapping (thousands of meters on one spool). I packed the barrels tight and built DIY shower filters: water in at the top, trickle down through strapping, clear out the bottom. Primitive, but effective—and in the basement we never battled algae, even with the sun.

> *LESSON:*   *Recyclers or architectural salvage stores are gold mines for all kinds of materials useful for DIYers.*

Food-safe barrels, odd fittings, sturdy odds-and-ends—cheap, reusable, perfect for DIY filtration.

The Science: The Weight of Water

Water doesn't look heavy—but it's one of the densest, most powerful forces you'll ever try to contain.

1 cubic foot of water weighs 62.4 lbs (28.3 kg).

1,000 gallons of water weighs over 8,300 lbs (3,765 kg)—more than a pickup truck.

A 3,000-gallon pond presses down with over 12 tons of weight.

This is why stacked concrete blocks alone are never enough. Water pressure will find every weakness, bow out walls, and exploit any gap. Reinforcement isn't optional; it's survival.

> *LESSON:*   *Build for water as if it's a living, moving giant—because it is.*

The Sandbag Summer

When spring returned, I stood at the lip of that cavern and asked, Where do I even start? The answer came from the news: spring floods on the Ottawa River; the Canadian Army sandbagging the banks. Sandbags—that's it.

7 - Sandbags as a foundation

I hunted down and found poly woven bags like the Army suggested and had 600 sandbags delivered. I started shoveling. (Our "sand shovels" were souvenir buys from Old Orchard Beach—small enough to lift full loads without breaking your back, nimble enough to maneuver in a pit.)

It was July. Bright sun on pure white sand, south-facing, made it as hot as the Sahara at the bottom of that hole. I filled bag after bag, cinched them tight with cable ties, dragged them into place, and stacked them nine high. At roughly 100 pounds each, the wall took shape—sturdy, unyielding. Jim planted a beach umbrella in the crater and set a cooler of beer beneath it. Somewhere there's a photo of me sitting on that cooler under the umbrella, sandbag walls towering around me.

The shape evolved as I worked. I stacked bags into stairs into one side so I could climb in and out. I built shelves on the broad end for future plant pockets. From above, the outline looked a bit like Mickey Mouse—two side lobes and a big round head.

> LESSON: *Sandbags make excellent structural walls against clay. Sandbags, when stacked properly, lock together, don't budge, and let you sculpt stairs, shelves, and curves.*

They're not UV-protected, though—so I had to keep them covered with underlayment or scraps of EPDM.

Drains, Lines, and "If You're Not a Fan of Backbreaking Work..."

The contractor had "forgotten" bottom drains. I wasn't making that mistake twice. Money was tight and 4-inch PVC was hard to source then, so I ran two 3-inch ABS lines instead, each with aerated drain covers. I trench-cut the clay bottom (hard going), set the drains, and ran the pipes straight to the far end, then up outside the sandbag wall to temporary standpipes.

23

> LESSON: *Bottom drains aren't strictly*
> *necessary—but they're your best friend if*
> *you hate backbreaking maintenance. They*
> *carry waste out before it decomposes.*

Inside the future filter area, I tied the standpipes into my *Frankenfilter* maze—returns, valves, mismatched fittings, here-there-everywhere. One visitor glanced at it and said, "Boy, I'd be scared of a leak." Fair.

Wrestling the Liner

Firestone generously donated a 50×50-foot EPDM liner (we just paid shipping). The roll weighed 700 pounds and was dumped at the curb. We couldn't budge it. My brother had an idea and flagged down a backhoe operator nearby on a build site. Fifty bucks and a case of beer later, the liner sat in our yard.

Six neighbors helped us fan-unfold it (whoever engineered that fold deserves a medal). The sheet covered the entire backyard like a ship's sail. We heaved and shuffled until it draped over the sandbag walls.

Then came the scariest cut: holes for the bottom drains. I must have read the order a dozen times—base plate, silicone, gasket, silicone, liner, silicone, top plate, screws, silicone—and used a full tube of sealant per drain. They never leaked. The wall return bulkhead went halfway up; I left the liner slightly loose around it so the sandbag behind could support the fitting without stressing the membrane.

The Four-Day Fill

We ran two hoses (front and back) for four days. As the water rose, I waded in and smoothed the folds so every wrinkle lay in the direction of the planned counter-clockwise current. Here's where I learned another trick:

> LESSON: *Tape down liner folds with two-sided EPDM*
> *seam tape. If you don't, debris can collect*
> *behind them—and small fish can get*
> *trapped*

We filled the pond to a foot below grade. The water line sat below grade because the yard hadn't been finished by the builder; we didn't yet know the final height. For now, "below grade" would have to do.

Then we waited.

We left the pond full over winter as a stress test—watching for wall movement, tears, any hint of failure. Spring arrived…and nothing had shifted.

We were good to go.

That summer, 2004, we carried koi up from the basement in Rubbermaid tubs and released them into real sunlight for the first time in nearly two years. They flashed gold, white, and red beneath the surface. A few leapt clean out of the water as if to declare, You did it. We're home.

Always use equipment sized correctly for your pond.

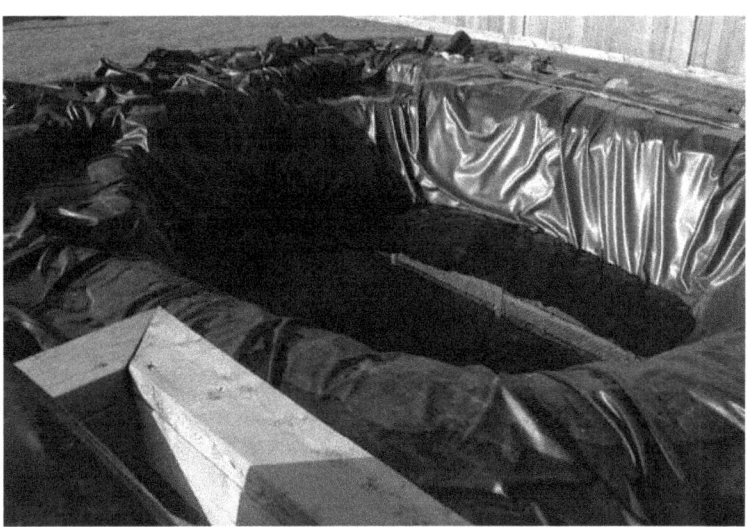

8 - Filling the pond - take 2

The Fish Return to the World

Spring 2004. Another thaw, another chance at redemption.

The water had sat all winter in the pond, untouched and unfiltered. The filters were still in the basement, hooked up to the temporary indoor tank where our koi had survived the long freeze. We waited until the outside water warmed enough, then it was moving day.

Easier said than done.

9 - *Releasing the fish*

There were a lot of fish by now, and some of them were getting big. We'd catch a few at a time, carry them upstairs in Rubbermaid tubs, and release them into the pond. They swam out like they'd been set free in the ocean, circling, leaping, flashing silver in the sunlight.

Yes, koi jump—especially in a new place, when they're testing boundaries. It reminded me of whales spyhopping, poking their heads up to look around.

It took hours to move them all. The last few fought us, darting between the net and the tub until Jim was red-faced and swearing. But eventually every fish was in the pond—sleek, strong, and finally back where they belonged.

We dismantled the Frankenfilter and hauled it outside. It sat on the mud at the pond's edge, ugly as sin—running, but woefully inadequate for a pond of 20,000 gallons. The surviving water plants went into the pockets I'd built into the walls, and to my surprise they thrived.

We were back in business. Sort of.

That summer, we kept tinkering. The filter pit was next. If the Frankenfilter was going to stay, it needed a home. I'd been reading about settling tanks and thought I could build one myself. Off we went to Cohen's again, and I came home with two 50-gallon food-grade barrels. I cut the tops, plumbed them into the bottom drains with 3-inch pipe, and hoped nature would help with the swirling flow.

It worked—sort of. The water moved, but balancing flow without overflowing the barrels was a constant fight. My plumbing knowledge at the time could fit in a thimble. I didn't know it yet, but I was about to earn a whole new set of lessons.

10 - *The Frankenfilter*

For now, though, we were just happy the koi were outside again. The water went green in two weeks—pea soup, and stayed green for the whole summer—but the fish didn't mind. They had room to grow, and we had another year to figure it out.

In one Canadian summer, we managed through hard work, to mitigate that disaster and have the fish back in their pond with an albeit deficient filter. It was a milestone really, that it looked as good as it did.

The war on filtration would come next. We had to do something better than our Frankenfilter.

The Science: Plumbing

Use the largest pipes you can afford. A 20,000-gallon pond with 1.5" plumbing is like trying to drink a milkshake through a cocktail straw.

Never use corrugated "pool hose." It kinks, leaks, and won't seal properly. Flexible PVC pipe is the gold standard.

Avoid 90° elbows. Every sharp turn kills water flow. Use gentle sweeps instead.

Plan for maintenance. Install unions and valves so you can remove or isolate every piece of equipment without draining your pond.

Budget early. Filtration and plumbing will eat at least half your pond budget. DIY what you can, but buy pro-grade for the core system.

The Koi Dome

Not to be confused with the Thunderdome, the Koi Dome was our salvation that first terrifying winter when we finally decided to leave the fish outdoors. Ottawa is no friend to koi keepers: frost routinely drives four feet into the ground. In my anxious imagination, that meant the fish would only have two feet of livable water left. (I didn't quite understand it back then, but the fear was real.)

We needed a plan.

Luckily, Clarke Koi in Toronto had published clear instructions for building a greenhouse over a pond—a simple frame of rebar, bent PVC pipe, and greenhouse sheeting. Unfortunately, they had never considered a 25 foot long, 16 foot wide pond. We followed their guide to the letter, documenting every step. Jim hammered rebar stakes into the ground at a 45° angle, and we slid PVC over top, bowing it into hoops across the pond. Another length of pipe served as the ridge spine. Once the skeleton stood, we rolled out greenhouse plastic from the local feed store and pulled it across the arches, weighing it down with patio stones, leftover pavers, and any heavy rocks we could scavenge.

The result was… odd, but effective. Our pond wasn't symmetrical, so one side of the dome stood tall while the other sloped low and flat. We would soon discover why that mattered.

11 - *Buried in snow*

Winter Battles

That winter dumped snow by the ton. Every storm pressed down harder on the dome, especially on that flat slope. Jim would dash outside with a broom, sweeping furiously to lighten the load. Each time he struck, the PVC hoops rebounded like giant springs, booming against the air. It sounded like a drumline in the backyard.

From the street, neighbors must have thought we'd built some kind of spaceship.

Still, the fish were safe. Inside the Koi Dome, the small volume of trapped air stayed surprisingly warm. The pond surface never froze, and the water never dropped below 40°F. For koi, that was a gentle winter.

The Miracle of February

By mid-February, we noticed something remarkable. The sun, higher and stronger, began to turn our makeshift dome into a true greenhouse. Outside, the backyard lay buried under drifts that piled up two feet high against the plastic walls. Inside, it was a different world.

The air beneath the dome was like early summer, 72F. The water followed, rising steadily until, by St. Patrick's Day, the koi were basking in summer conditions.

We'd crawl inside on our hands and knees, dressed in ski gear, only to strip off jackets and sit there in T-shirts, laughing at the absurdity of it all. It felt like stepping through a portal—winter raging outside, summer alive beneath the plastic arch.

The koi responded in kind. After two years in a basement tank and one disastrous pond start, they were finally thriving. They swam lazily in the warmth, sleek and strong, utterly oblivious to the snow piled seven feet high on the fence beyond.

12 - Relaxing with the fish

A Backyard Attraction

Our pond had become a neighborhood novelty. Kids came to peer through the fence at the fish, and our own children waded and even swam with them. The koi seemed to enjoy human company; whenever someone slipped into the water, they would school around, brushing arms and legs with curious confidence.

We were "the house with the fish." And our fish were only just getting started.

Because by the time spring arrived, our koi decided to thank us for their winter home with a gift we hadn't anticipated—a full-on spawning riot that turned our carefully nurtured pond into a frothing, splashing battlefield of fins and eggs.

The Science: The Frost Line Isn't the Same as Pond Depth

In places like Ottawa, frost can drive four feet into the ground—which sounds terrifying if your pond is six feet deep. It feels like the ice might push right down into the fish's space.

But soil and water behave differently. Soil freezes solid because it's static. Water resists freezing because it constantly circulates heat, and it's slow to cool. Even in severe winters, ice rarely penetrates more than 12–18 inches into a pond. The water below stays liquid, buffered by the Earth's warmth.

LESSON: *A four-foot frost line doesn't mean you'll lose four feet of pond. Water has its own built-in insulation.*

The Science: How the Greenhouse Dome Worked

Your dome acted like a giant cold-frame greenhouse. The clear plastic trapped solar energy and stopped wind from stripping heat away.

Even just a few inches of air gap under the dome acted as insulation—air is a poor conductor of heat, so it slowed heat loss from the water. Snow piled on top actually helped by adding another insulating layer, like a blanket.

This created a microclimate: cold outside, but warm and stable inside. The air warmed into the 70°Fs, and the water followed, never dropping below 40°F—perfect for overwintering koi.

31

The Science: Why Koi Spawned in Spring

As the water warmed, the koi's biology responded. Temperature controls almost everything about their metabolism and behaviour.

Once water rises above about 68 °F, koi become fully active. Warmer water also triggers their reproductive cycle—especially after a cold dormant period. To them, the rising temperature and increasing daylight signaled: "Spring is here. Time to spawn."

13 - *Spawning fish*

The Frankenfilter Flush

Our first spring with fish overwintered outside taught us a lesson we never forgot: pond filters don't hibernate clean.

We had built what I can only call the Frankenfilter—oversized, inefficient, and prone to building up sludge faster than we could flush it out. After a winter of sitting idle, it had quietly transformed into a sewage factory. By April, the water inside was black, heavy with ammonia and hydrogen sulfide, and stank like a cross between a swamp and a septic tank.

Note: We did not run the filters once the water temperature went below 45°F(8°C).

14 - *PandVac booked up to filters*

The first time we cracked it open, the odor rolled out like a fog. Hydrogen sulfide has that unmistakable "rotten egg" smell, but when mixed with fish waste and decaying organics, it graduates to "dead body." Honestly, I'm still surprised an NCIS film crew didn't show up with crime scene tape when we backwashed that thing.

We knew we couldn't let that brew drain back into the pond—it would have killed the koi on the spot. So we "innovated": we ran a line of 3-inch ABS pipe from the basement sewer clean out all the way out to the filter area. Then we hooked up our PondVac (a great device, by the way) and sent the sludge straight to the sewer where it belonged.

Getting the pumps going meant setting the filters to "backwash" and standing well back while they belched out thick, nose-curling gloop. It was awful, but also oddly satisfying. Every gallon that went down the pipe was one less chance of disaster in the pond.

LESSON: *Never recycle filter sludge into your pond. Build a bypass or waste line if you can. Your fish will thank you, and you won't have to explain to your neighbors why your backyard smells like a crime drama set.*

The Science: Hydrogen Sulfide

If you've ever opened a filter after winter and been knocked back by the stench of rotten eggs, you've met hydrogen sulfide (H_2S).

Where it comes from: When organic sludge (fish waste, leaves, food) breaks down in oxygen-starved zones of a pond or filter, anaerobic bacteria take over. Their byproduct is H_2S gas.

Why it smells so bad: Just a few parts per million are enough for that nose-curling "septic" odor. In higher concentrations, it smells like death—literally, because it's toxic.

Why it's dangerous: H_2S interferes with oxygen transport in fish blood, leading to suffocation even in well-oxygenated water. A single backwash of sludge water into a pond can kill fish within minutes.

How to avoid it:

- Never let sludge-filled water back flow into the pond.
- If your filter sits idle over winter, always flush the filter to waste before shutting down.

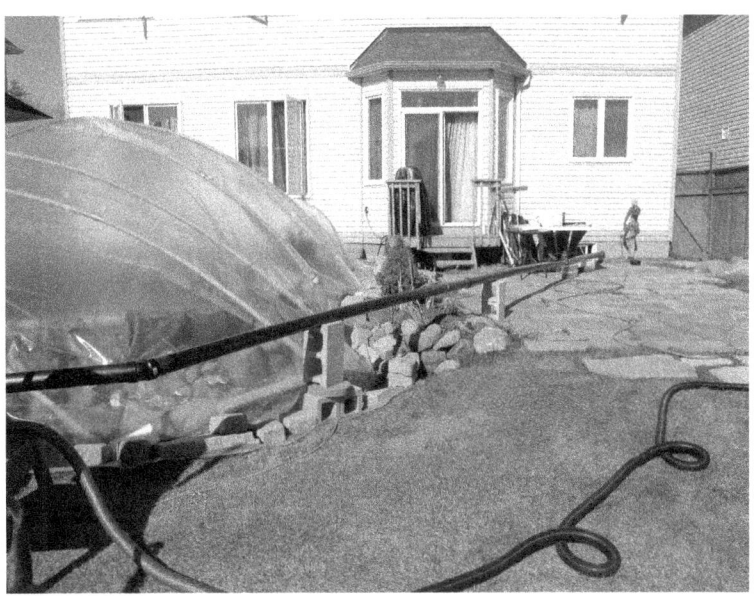

15 - *Hook up to sewage in house*

LESSON: *Hydrogen sulfide is a silent killer. If it*
smells like rotten eggs, treat it like sewage.
Vent it away and keep it out of your pond.

Frisky Fish

The summer of 2005 had already been busy—building walls around the pond, keeping the fish healthy, and starting the shed. But just as we thought we had things under control, the fish surprised us with one more event: spawning.

No one had told me that spawning was a contact sport—as rough and rowdy as Australian rules football. That first morning, all we knew was that there was water splashing everywhere. Our carefully corralled plants, secured in laundry baskets with pool-noodle floaties, were being tossed upside down, plants strewn out of the water like a battlefield.

LESSON: *Koi are omnivores. If they can wrap their lips around it, they'll eat it. Bugs, shrimp, flowers—even a cat's tail if it dangles too close. Keeping plants alive in a koi pond is a challenge.*

My laundry basket contraption had worked well up until then. The plants thrived inside their floating cages, safe from hungry mouths. But that summer morning, the baskets became playthings in a frenzy I hadn't anticipated.

A female koi tore around the pond, four or five males chasing her like a pack of rugby forwards. Whenever they cornered her, they rammed her sides with their noses, jostling and pummeling. I stood open-mouthed—this was spawning? I had pictured a delicate ballet: a female releasing eggs, males fertilizing them in turn. Instead, it was an aquatic bar brawl.

Research later confirmed what I had witnessed: koi spawning is rough, exhausting, and sometimes dangerous for females. Professional breeders often keep males and females separate for exactly that reason. But I didn't have the facilities for

A single female koi can lay half a million eggs. Half a million. Even if only 1% survive, that's still 5,000 fry—and each of those fry grows into a one-meter fish.

37

that, so my only option was to monitor the chaos and be ready with a quarantine tank if injuries happened.

And then came the vast numbers of eggs. Suddenly the problem became clear. The advice I found (and followed): was 'let the adults eat the spawn.'

So we stopped feeding the fish. They happily feasted on fresh caviar for a week. Still, eggs clung everything: to plants, to the laundry baskets, to the liner, even on the stones above the waterline.

By day three, the pond water foamed with froth, smelled "off," and ammonia levels spiked from zero to 2.0 ppm. For years I'd been told any detectable ammonia was toxic—yet here were my koi happily making more of it. I panicked.

It was clear: I needed to scale up my capacity to store products to fix problems. Pondkeeping in Canada wasn't just about filters and hoses—it was about stocking supplies on a pond-sized scale. Products from the pet store were laughable: one capful of ammonia neutralizer for 10 gallons? That meant 25 bottles for my 20,000-gallon pond.

Eventually, I found Seachem Prime, a concentrated conditioner where one 5 ml dose treats 2,000 gallons. I started buying two-liter bottles at $72 a pop, and when trouble struck, I dumped the whole thing in. Expensive, yes—but essential.

> LESSON: *You need to have ample supplies on hand at all times to deal with emergencies. Neutralizing ammonia spikes means having more than a "normal" dose.*

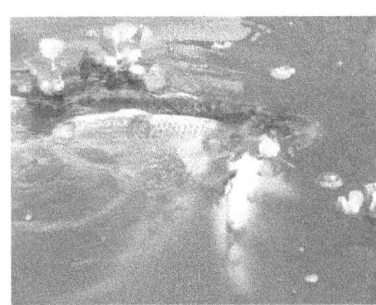

16 - *Caesar is a girl?*

Another way of dealing with ammonia spikes due to spawning is to do a water change. For us, a 10% change on a 20,000-gallon pond is 2,000 gallons. That's not just running the garden hose for a few minutes—that's like drawing down a municipal water system. Plan ahead, and don't wait until you're in crisis to realize you don't have enough supply.

Finally, one more reminder: protect your pond from runoff. Even a single rainstorm washing lawn chemicals or heavy metals into your water can wipe out every fish in hours. Elevate pond edges above ground level to keep the outside world outside.

> LESSON: *Elevate your pond edges above ground level. Never, ever allow ground runoff.*

The chaos of spawning lasted over a week. Every morning, more eggs, more froth, and more exhausted females. But as breeders say, "the fastest and the strongest survive." Out of an estimated three million eggs from five or six females, about 30 fry made it. Tiny sticks with eyes darted among the baskets, quick as lightning, hiding from the big mouths.

In the middle of all this chaos, we had one more surprise waiting for us. Our big, beautiful male—Caesar—the one we always admired for his size and presence—suddenly revealed "he" was a she. During spawning, it became undeniable.

"Oh my gosh," I remember blurting out. "She's a girl!"

Well, Caesar didn't care. She kept right on being magnificent, strutting (or splashing) around the pond while the others chased and bumped. Her name stuck—Caesar she was, Caesar she remained. But from that day on, we couldn't help but smile whenever we called her name.

Don't assume the sex of your koi, learn how to check and know rather than guess.

For weeks they schooled separately, fry zipping as a pack and even stealing food from the adults. By the time they reached two inches, the big koi stopped chasing them and accepted them into the larger school.

Curiously, that was the only time our koi ever spawned. I've often wondered if it was because after that, they were all family. Koi aren't known for incest taboos—but perhaps even fish have their limits.

By Thanksgiving, the fry were still darting about, but our attention had turned to the looming Ottawa winter. Jim decided this year's koi dome would be taller, larger, and cover the shed as well. That sounded like a good idea... but we hadn't realized that without a proper spine, this dome would present a whole new set of problems.

But that's another story.

Pond-Keeping at Scale

Managing water quality with additives is not new. Walk into any aquarium store and you'll see shelves filled with products promising to fix pH, bind ammonia, clear cloudy water. They're all designed for aquariums—10, 20, maybe 50 gallons at most.

A pond is another world entirely. Not because it's chemically different, but because it's bigger. The scale makes all the difference.

Take salt, for example. At the pet store, you'll find aquarium salt sold in little 2-quart cartons for $5.99. That might work for a guppy tank. But if you need to dose a 3,000-gallon pond? A maintenance dose alone (1 lb per 1,000 gallons) means three pounds. A therapeutic dose could be ten times that. Suddenly, you'd be hauling home 40 cartons. Ridiculous.

The same math applies to ammonia neutralizers. Pet store brands are packaged in 250 ml or 500 ml bottles—one capful for 10 gallons. For my 20,000-gallon pond, that meant twenty-five bottles just to handle one spawning spike. Not practical, not affordable.

The lesson I learned: buy at scale. Pond suppliers, fish farms, and wholesalers sell pond-sized products at concentrations that make sense. A few examples:

Seachem Prime – A 500 ml bottle treats 2,000 gallons. For ponds, buy it by the liter or two-liter jug so you actually have enough on hand. When trouble strikes, you need to be able to dose immediately, not after a trip to the store.

Chloram-X – A dry powder that neutralizes ammonia and chloramine. Available in large tubs, perfect for pond keepers.

Pond salt – Skip the aquarium cartons. Go to the hardware store and buy bulk non-iodized salt. Sea salt is the best, Morton's has both in bulk packs.

Baking soda – is an essential to have on hand to keep up the carbonate in the water. Carbonate is a key food source for the bacteria that clean your water.

Try out my handy-dandy Pond Calculator Google Sheet. I've got a pond volume calculator, as well as some doseages for basic meds like salt and dechlorinator products.

The Science: A Word About Salt

Salt is one of the most versatile and important tools for koi keepers. It reduces stress, combats nitrite toxicity, and supports gill function. But confusion abounds about which type of salt to use. Let's clear the water:

What Kind of Salt?

- **Rock Salt** (water softener type, non-pelletized) – Safe and effective if it is pure sodium chloride (NaCl) with no additives such as anti-caking agents, rust inhibitors, or binders. This has been a staple for decades.

- **Sea Salt** – Also sodium chloride, with small amounts of minerals like magnesium and calcium. Often marketed as essential, but the benefits are marginal and largely unnecessary in a well-managed pond.

- **Aquarium/Pond Salt** – Pure NaCl sold under aquarium brands. Convenient, but usually the most expensive option.

Bottom line: As long as it is additive-free, plain salt is plain salt. There is no requirement to use "sea salt."

How to Add Salt

Never dump a large amount directly into the pond. Sudden concentration changes shock fish and filter bacteria. Instead:

- Dissolve salt in a bucket of pond water before adding it, or

- Place solid salt chunks in a high-flow area such as the waterfall, so it dissolves gradually.

This ensures even distribution and a safe, steady rise in salinity.

The Science: Common Salt Treatments

Purpose	Salt %	Metric Dose	Imperial Dose
General tonic stress relief	0.1-0.3%	1-3 kg per 1000 L	0.83-2.5 lb per 264 US gal
Nitrite spike protection	0.6%	6 kg per 1000 L	5 lb per 264 US gal
Parasite treatment (short-term bath)	1.0-1.5%	10-15 kg per 1000 L	8.3-12.5 lb per 264 US gal

Quick conversion tip:
1000 L ≈ 264 US gallons
1 kg ≈ 2.2 lb

PRO TIP: *Always dissolve salt fully before adding it to the pond, and never add salt if using formalin or potassium permanganate treatments—they can react dangerously*

with salt. Always measure salinity with a reliable test before and after dosing.

Key Point: A single water change doesn't "dilute" salt—it reduces concentration in exact proportion to the water removed.

50% water change → cuts salt level in half.

Two 50% changes in a row → leaves salt at 25% of the original level.

Three 50% changes → leaves just 12.5% of the original.

PRO TIP: *Salt Stays Until You Remove It: Unlike some treatments, salt doesn't break down or disappear. Once added, it remains in the pond until it is physically removed with water changes.*

Always record salt additions and water changes in your pond log for accurate tracking. This is why it's essential to measure salinity before re-dosing. Adding more salt without accounting for what's still in the pond can quickly overshoot safe levels.

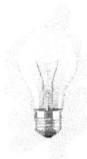

PRO TIP: *Always add salt to your pond in moving water. Rock salt dissolving slowly in the waterfall provides a steady, controlled dose—a method trusted by experienced koi keepers.*

𝒯𝒽𝑒 𝒮𝒸𝒾𝑒𝓃𝒸𝑒: "But Koi Are Freshwater Fish..."

True—koi and goldfish evolved in freshwater, not the ocean. But that doesn't mean they live salt-free.

All water has minerals. Even freshwater contains dissolved salts in small amounts. Rivers and lakes naturally carry sodium, calcium, and other ions that fish rely on.

Fish physiology: Koi constantly fight a battle to keep salts inside their bodies from leaking out into the surrounding water. This balancing act consumes energy and becomes harder under stress. A small amount of added salt makes that job easier.

Emergency buffer: Salt is also unique in protecting against nitrite poisoning and easing osmotic stress when fish are sick or injured.

So while koi don't need ocean levels of salt, the right dose of plain sodium chloride can be life-saving.

LESSON: *Salt isn't about making freshwater fish into saltwater fish. It's about giving koi a safety net their natural rivers and ponds already provide in trace amounts. It's your first line of defense against Nitrite poisoning or Brown Blood Disease.*

KH is your pond's safety net. Without it, pH goes on a roller coaster ride driven by algae and daily light cycles. With it, your water stays stable, your bacteria thrive, and your koi avoid dangerous stress.

Five things to have on hand

20 - *Baking Soda*

23 - *Seachem F*

22 - *Seachem Stability*

24 - *Pond Salt*

21 - *ChlorAm-X*

The Science: Carbonate Hardness—The Pond's Buffer

In pond keeping, stability is everything. The measure that gives you that stability is carbonate hardness (KH)—the pond's buffering capacity.

What KH Does
- KH is made up of carbonate and bicarbonate dissolved in the water.
- These compounds act as a buffer, absorbing acids and keeping pH steady.
- KH also serves as food for the beneficial bacteria that drive the nitrogen cycle.
- During nitrification, bacteria use about 7.14 mg of alkalinity (as calcium carbonate / $CaCO$) for every 1 mg of ammonia they process.

If KH runs out, those bacteria slow down or stop working, and your pH can crash.

The KH–Algae–pH Cycle
- KH doesn't just affect bacteria—it also connects directly to algae growth and daily pH swings:
- Daytime: Algae photosynthesize, consuming carbon dioxide and pulling carbonates (KH) out of the water. With less CO2 available, pH rises.
- Nighttime: Algae release CO2 back into the water, which lowers pH.
- Low KH: Without a strong buffer, these daily swings become extreme, stressing fish and destabilizing filters.
- Algae blooms: Heavy blooms can burn through KH shockingly fast, setting the stage for a sudden acid crash when the bloom dies off.

Maintaining the Buffer
- Test KH regularly with a drop kit
- Aim for 150–200 ppm (about 8–11 drops with API test) in a koi pond
- Use plain sodium bicarbonate (baking soda) to raise KH safely and gradually.

The Mega Dome Massacre

November Winds Toss Boulders like Cookies

Winter was coming, and after the success of our first dome we thought we'd learned enough to improve the design. The plan was ambitious: a Mega Dome, taller, longer, and wide enough to cover not only the pond but also the new filter shed.

There was one flaw. It was so big we couldn't put in a central spine, and that would prove to be fatal.

Jim went off to a convention in Florida (to an amusement park magazine, in the land of Disney), leaving me alone to watch over our masterpiece. Naturally, that's when a November storm rolled in.

I stood at the kitchen door watching the dome turn into a sail. The wind came roaring over the house, slammed down on the plastic, and compressed the dome until it looked like a giant hand was pressing on it. Then the pipes would spring back up, exploding with sonic booms that rattled the windows.

When one corner tore loose, the wind picked up a 16-foot 2x12 plank and tossed it—plus the boulders weighing it down—across the lawn like they were Lego blocks. I ran outside in rain and razor-stinging wind, trying to wrestle the board back into the plastic, chasing rocks as they bounced across the yard.

> "The wind would slam down the dome, then it went BOOM like a sonic cannon."

That's when Jim called. From sunny Florida. With palm trees swaying around him.

"Hi, how are you doing?" he asked cheerfully.

I yelled into the phone, "I'M A LITTLE BUSY RIGHT NOW!"

No photo could capture the sight: me, soaked and staggering, clinging to plastic and rocks while the dome roared like a drum. But it's burned into my memory.

45

February 7, 2006: The Collapse

If November was chaos, January was catastrophe. While we were away during Christmas break, my brother offered to keep a watch on the fish and our cats.

It snowed. A lot. In fact, we got 50 cm (20 inches) in one dumping. It was one of the heaviest snowfalls on record.

Well, our Mega dome didn't fare too well. Remember the fact we didn't put in a ridge pole? Yeah, this is when it made a difference. Without that center support, all the poles did the splits. That left huge gaps between each one, where nothing held up the snow.

So the inevitable happened. The entire top of the dome collapsed inside the walls and was sitting on the surface of the pond.

25 - *Fireplace inside dome*

My brother valiantly tried to prevent it. He even spent a night inside the dome heating it with the portable outdoor propane fireplace. But when that showed signs of becoming too hot on the plastic, he had to stop.

There was nothing my brother could do, but look on in dismay.

When we got home it was waiting for us, a caldera of snow on top of the pond.

Our friend Helder came over to help Jim because this was clearly not a job for one man. They stood around and scratched their heads until Jim came up with the idea of floating a queen-sized air mattress on the pond.

Jim would use the mattress to float to the middle of the pond and then use it as a platform to shovel out the snow and ice. So there he was, bundled like a woolly mammoth, belly-crawling across the air mattress with a shovel.

> **"I was chasing boulders across the yard while Jim called from sunny Florida."**

With every chunk of ice he removed, the poles groaned and shifted. Just as he cleared the last big piece, the entire structure rebounded, exploding upward with a boom that sent ice and snow flying 20 feet into the air. Jim barely scrambled off in time to avoid being catapulted into the neighbor's yard. It was like watching the pond itself reject winter.

Aftermath

By February, the dome looked like a war zone. The PVC hoops were crooked and bent, ropes sagged, and the once-proud Mega Dome stood like a broken old man. Still standing but barely. The last thing it needed was another wind storm, but it got one.

The final blow came a few weeks later. The wind started howling at 7:00 that morning. I got up and looked out a second story window and watched the wind drumming the dome. You know the song BOOM chakalaka BOOM. But there's no chakalaka...

I screamed at Jim to get up and flew downstairs as fast as I could and jumped into outer clothes and tore outside. I heard a horrible sound and ran around to the far end, and spotted a two-foot tear in the plastic. I grabbed the flapping edge and held on for dear

> **"With one final zzzzzzip, the Mega Dome unzipped itself end to end."**

life, but the wind drummed again, compressing the entire structure until it exploded back up again.

Jim finally arrived, saw what I was doing and took up a position beside me, also holding together on two edges. But it didn't matter, a second later there was a terrible zzzzzzzzzzzzipping sound as the tear ran the entire length of the dome, opening 50 feet of plastic in three seconds. The wind flipped the plastic top clean off the dome and into the air to land in the neighbor's yard.

26 - *A broken pond cover*

We were standing there, still holding onto plastic shreds, as it was so fast we didn't have time to move. The wind stung my eyes with cold ice pellets until I was squinting. Jim suddenly went into overdrive, running after the loose plastic flapping, and threatening to knock down even more. While he was wrestling with it to roll it up, I, as fast as I could, got two pond de-icers and deployed them, one on each end. Then I ran to get the air pump from the basement, and dropped two small airstones into the pond and put the pump in the shed.

The water started freezing within half an hour. The plants that had suddenly been exposed were devastated, and crushed. The fish went deep. But one was too close to the surface and I worried about him.

The fish had survived until then, but with the pond suddenly exposed to -4°F (-20°C) weather they were at risk. The water surface was completely frozen within hours, catching several koi by surprise. We lost many of our originals that winter.

It was heartbreaking. The Mega Dome had protected them, even if imperfectly, and its failure hit hard.

In March, we decided to cover the pond again. There was more sun now, and we shortened the poles. Even a partial cover helped warm the water up faster.

The next cover would have to be better, smarter, and safer. The lesson was written in PVC and plastic—and in the memory of the fish we lost.

> **LESSON:** *Bigger domes need more structure. Always include a rigid ridge pole or truss system to keep the arches from doing the splits.*

The Science: Snow Load Adds Up Fast

Ottawa snow is heavy—about 20–25 pounds per cubic foot (320–400 kg/m³) when wet. A single storm can dump 50 cm (20 inches), which adds up shockingly fast.

For example, just 10 m² (107 ft²) of roof area with 50 cm (20") of wet snow weighs over 1,800 kg (nearly 2 tons) pressing down on the structure.

Without proper framing, that weight can crush PVC arches flat—especially if the snow partially melts, turns to slush, then refreezes into ice.

> **LESSON:** *Any winter dome must be engineered to support thousands of pounds of potential snow load.*

27 - Spring cover helped warm water

The Science: Oxygen Under Ice—Why a Hole Matters

In winter, ponds can freeze over completely. To us, that looks peaceful—but for the fish below, a solid ice cap is dangerous.

Gas exchange stops: When ice seals the pond, oxygen can't enter and carbon dioxide can't escape. Other gases, like methane and hydrogen sulfide, also build up under the ice.

Fish suffocation risk: Even in cold water, koi and goldfish still need oxygen. Without exchange, dissolved oxygen levels slowly fall, sometimes fatally.

Why holes help: A small open hole in the ice allows gases to vent and fresh oxygen to enter. It doesn't have to be large—just enough for air and water to "breathe."Aeration beats heaters:

Aerators keep water moving, preventing ice from forming around the bubbles. They also pull up slightly warmer water from below, circulating oxygen.

De-icers (heaters) work too, but they use more electricity than air pumps and can freeze in extreme cold.

LESSON: *If a pond cover fails in midwinter, act immediately to keep part of the surface open with aeration or de-icers. Even a small opening can save the whole pond.*

The Science: Why Sudden Exposure is Deadly

When the greenhouse dome tore open, our koi were suddenly exposed to −4°F (−20°C) air.

Ponds lose heat mainly from the surface. When the dome vanished, the warm water met cold air and began freezing within hours. Fish trapped near the surface were hit by a double shock:

Rapid temperature drop

Sudden oxygen loss as the surface sealed over with ice

This combination can trigger winterkill—mass death caused by cold stress and oxygen depletion.

28 - *Inside the Mega Dome*

I'm Not Saying It's Aliens ....

After the unzipping of the Mega Dome, the weather went feral. Snow came sideways, the wind cut like knives, and the temperature plunged to -4°F (-20°C) in a single afternoon. The pond, which had been cruising along at a cozy 51°F (10°C) under the dome, suddenly faced air thirty degrees colder. The result: a flash freeze.

29 - De-icer overcome by ice

Nothing we deployed—two de-icers, two air stones, and a pump stashed in the shed—to help the fish, worked as advertised. The heaters froze into the ice almost immediately, like toys abandoned in a slushy drink. The aerators fared better, but they still couldn't keep up with the cold. Still they created a steady stream of bubbles that broke the surface.

And then something very strange happened. The bubbles began to freeze as they surfaced. Instead of breaking, they stacked. A delicate lattice of ice foam built itself higher and higher. Day by day, the structure grew taller, until a bizarre spire nearly three feet high loomed over the pond.

It looked less like pond equipment and more like a prop from The X-Files. In the photos, it glows against the snow like some living creature crawling out of the water. We nicknamed it The Pond Alien—and for weeks, it stood sentinel over the koi, a surreal sculpture made entirely of frozen breath.

LESSON: *Aeration is your best defense in extreme cold—but in Canadian winters, don't be surprised if nature decides to sculpt her own strange monuments in your backyard.*

LESSON: *In winter, it's not about heating the pond—it's about keeping it breathing. One open hole in the ice can make the difference between a healthy spring and a pond full of dead fish.*

The Science: Biofilm & Beneficial Bacteria

A healthy pond isn't "clean" in the sterile sense. It's alive—balanced by billions of microscopic workers you can't see.

Who they are: Beneficial bacteria that colonize every surface—liner, rocks, filter media, even pipes. They form a slimy coating called biofilm.

What they do: These bacteria are the backbone of the nitrogen cycle:

One group converts toxic ammonia (NH_3) from fish waste into nitrite (NO_2).

Another group converts nitrite into nitrate (NO_3), which is far less harmful and can be absorbed by plants.

Why it matters: Without this living filter, ammonia and nitrite spike to lethal levels. Clear water isn't safe water unless the bacteria are doing their job.

The danger of "too clean":

When you scrub your pond bare or sterilize your filters, you strip away the biofilm. It takes weeks for bacteria colonies to rebuild, leaving fish exposed to toxic water chemistry in the meantime.

The Science: Why Did the Pond Alien Form?

The "alien tower" wasn't magic—it was physics meeting extreme cold.

Supercooled air: At –20 °C, rising bubbles froze almost instantly on contact with the surface.

Film freezing: Instead of popping, the thin bubble walls solidified into fragile ice shells.

Stacking effect: Each new bubble pushed up beneath the frozen ones, welding more shells into place. Over hours and days, the column grew taller.

Foam lattice: Because the bubbles were full of air, the tower looked porous and spongy, more like frozen sea foam than solid ice.

This phenomenon is rare, but can happen wherever aeration meets bitter cold. It's the same principle that creates "ice volcanoes" on the shores of the Great Lakes—water plus wind plus freezing air, building strange sculptures nature never repeats the same way twice.

In other words: our pond didn't grow an alien. It grew science art.

LESSON: *Don't fight the slime. That slippery layer on your liner or filter isn't dirt—it's life support for your fish. Think of it as your pond's invisible workforce, working 24/7 for free.*

30 - *The pond alien "family"*

31 - *Helder inspecting the Pond Alien*

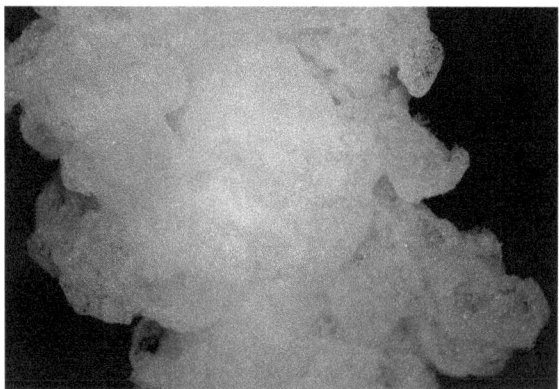

32 - *Close up of the frozen bubbles*

The Waterfall

The summer of 2006 brought us a bit of luck—and a lot of rock. We had met a young landscaper who claimed waterfalls were his specialty. Even better, we arranged a trade: a feature about him for *Koi World* magazine in exchange for his work on our pond. We had already gathered a fair pile of stone from neighboring empty lots and construction sites, so he was delighted to have materials to play with.

33 - *Rocks, stone, and dirt for the waterfall*

One piece in particular was monumental. We called it the *dragon's tooth*—a triangular boulder at least four feet long. We somehow managed to stand it upright on its blunt end, the point stabbing skyward. It looked so solid, it alone seemed to hold the pond wall in place. At the time, I had no clue how to make the pond edge look natural, but I knew these rocks were destined for more than a pile.

When our contractor arrived, he brought even more stone, gravel, and equipment. The first step was undoing much of the work we had done the year before. The block wall holding the liner came down, the water level dropped, and he installed a waterfall tank plumbed back to the filter shed. A skimmer and pump were added.

This way typical for us: *three steps forward, two steps backward*. It was the theme of our pond building. But then, we frequently affected a solution we knew at the time was temporary and would have to be redone at some point.

Once the plumbing was set, the artistry began. A truckload of dirt arrived, followed by heaps of river stone ranging from pebbles to hefty 5-inch cobbles. With these, he painted the landscape, layering textures and colors like brush strokes. Somehow, he even coaxed massive boulders to balance in place—stones that looked like they should topple any second but never did.

The most magical touch was his ear. He didn't just build a waterfall, he *tuned it*. By arranging and rearranging stones, he adjusted the sound until it sang the way he wanted. Water tumbled down two small steps, and the tone shifted from splash to tinkle to murmur. In the end, it sounded like a mountain brook—soft, soothing, never intrusive. Only a foot high, yet it filled the garden with peace.

When he finished, we had a water feature as beautiful as it was musical. My daughter adored it so much that she immediately pulled on her bathing suit, climbed into her inflatable boat, and floated among the koi as though she had her own water park. By then, the fry from the year before had grown to six inches, and the pond held about forty fish.

One thought loomed large: *we really need a better filter system.*

LESSON: *A waterfall is more than art. Done well, it's both a living sculpture and an oxygen machine. Done poorly, it can waste water and strain your system.*

The Science: Tuning A Waterfall

Waterfalls aren't just decoration—they shape how a ponds look, sound, and even breathe.

Tuning for Sound

- Flat slabs create sheets of water that fall in a steady curtain—smooth and quiet.
- Jagged stones break the flow into splashes—louder and more energetic.
- Stepped falls give a layered sound, from trickle to gurgle, depending on height and stone spacing.

A skilled builder will "tune" a waterfall like an instrument, adjusting rock placement until the sound fits the mood of the garden.

Oxygen Boost

As water tumbles and breaks apart, it pulls oxygen into the pond. This extra aeration supports koi, beneficial bacteria, and helps reduce stress during hot weather when oxygen levels drop.

The Hidden Cost

Waterfalls also increase evaporation and can splash out more water than you expect. If built too small or paired with an undersized filter, they'll add beauty but not enough circulation.

Design Tips

- Match the pump size to the width of the spillway (about 100 gph per inch of waterfall width for a nice sheet).
- Keep the waterfall height low—12–18 inches is usually plenty for sound and oxygen without over-splash.
- Direct the return flow toward open areas of the pond to keep water circulating evenly.

34 - *Final touches; ready to plant*

35 - *Tuning the waterfall*

36 - *Finished waterfall*

The Basement Pond Upgrade (2006)

A Sad Spring, A Big Decision

2006 began on a grim note. The cathedral dome had collapsed, and we were left with the heartbreaking task of netting out koi that hadn't survived the winter. It was awful, smelly work. We vowed not to put the survivors through another gamble.

That meant bringing the fish inside again for the 2006–2007 winter — and this time, the crowding made it impossible to ignore. The old basement pond was little more than a block canoe: leaky, bowed, and patched together. With that many growing koi jammed inside, it became crystal clear that if we were going to keep koi indoors, it needed to become a real pond — stronger, deeper, filtered, and properly plumbed for circulation.

> "If you look through your basement window from outside, it looks like your house is flooded—with fish," said Eric.

Enter Eric the Carpenter

Whenever we needed carpentry work done, we called Eric. He'd helped us on a number of projects, in both this house and our previous house. He felt like part of our family. He had finished the basement, built custom window-well covers for the cats, and even turned our living room into an office. He also liked to tease us about our "basement fish."

When we described the next "project", he laughed, shook his head, and got to work.

Eric's first verdict was blunt: *"If you're making this taller, the walls need serious reinforcement."* His solution was custom-milled angle iron, ¼" thick and four inches by four inches, bolted straight into the slab and walls. When he started drilling, the noise was deafening. The ladies working upstairs in my sewing business would ask, "What's Eric building now?"

Once the angle iron was in, the walls were solid. Eric added three more rows of blocks, filled with rebar and concrete. He grumbled the walls weren't plumb, but that wasn't his fault—it was ours from the "canoe" days. His solution was genius: clad the walls in cedar to make them look intentional, spa-like, and straight.

Working with Joe the Plumber

I wanted the "plumbing done right". So we hired someone. Joe came to us as a mid-twenties, unmarried, and eager Journeyman plumber—he arrived expecting a normal bathroom install. Instead, when we outlined our pond project, he didn't blink. He grinned from ear to ear.

Armed with a jackhammer, Joe tore into the basement slab to install two bottom drains. Each was finished slightly raised above the floor and surrounded by a hand-shaped bowl of concrete so waste would funnel down. He filled in the corners of the tank, rounding them with concrete so debris had nowhere to hide. For a plumber, his parging work was masterful.

> "Finally, something fun! We never get to build systems like this," said Joe.

Joe tied the drains into a 50-gallon food drum set up as a settling tank—this time correctly plumbed tangentially so water would swirl and solids drop out. And the best part? The whole system was tied into the waste line that was meant to be a bathroom rough-in. One pull of a knife valve and sludge went straight to the sewer. No more carrying buckets of stinky stuff.

PRO TIP: *Spend your money where it counts—on quality valves, unions, and Schedule 40 pressurized flexpipe. Use ABS on gravity-fed runs, and always bury your pipes below frost depth.*

Failures Along the Way

Of course, no pond project goes without a fiasco. We thought we'd be clever and try EPDM paint instead of a liner. On paper it made sense: sleek, seamless, easy to clean. In reality, it bubbled and peeled. The concrete was simply too new and too wet.

38 - Eric finishing cedar deck

I called the manufacturer. Their verdict: *"Concrete must cure for months before you coat it. Otherwise, the paint won't stick."*

Lesson learned. Out came the paint, and in went a heavy EPDM liner. Wrestling it into place was sweaty, awkward work—folds, corners, slippery rubber everywhere. It was "all hands on deck" for hours.

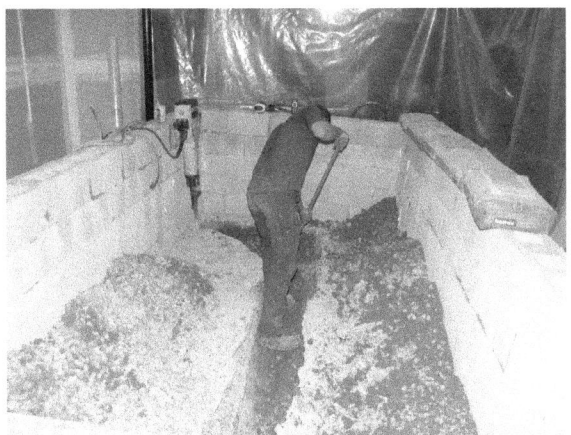

40 - *Joe digging a trench for the drain pupe*

39 - *Savvio Skimmer, Filter, and settling tank*

The Science: The Settling Tank Secret

A settling tank is just a barrel with brains. And for DIYers, it's a great tool to have in your filter system. Instead of filtering with pads or media, it uses time and physics:

•   Water swirls in.

•   Solids settle out.

•   Clearer water exits on top.

The key is to connect the pipe to the barrel tangentially. That means off center. This causes the swirling. The direction isn't random—it's caused by the Coriolis effect, the same force that makes weather systems spin. In the Northern Hemisphere, water tends to swirl counterclockwise; in the Southern Hemisphere, it spins clockwise.

That swirl acts like a slow-motion vortex. Heavier particles drop out of suspension, sliding to the bottom, while lighter, cleaner water moves on. Think of it as a tornado flipped upside down, doing quiet housework in your pond.

This is mechanical filtration—it removes physical waste. A biofilter, by contrast, uses bacteria to break down dissolved toxins like ammonia. Both are essential, but the settling tank does the "heavy lifting."

From Concrete Canoe to Cedar Spa

Once the liner was installed, Eric returned to finish the exterior of the tank. He built a cedar deck at one end and a raised deck along the back wall under the window, hiding pipes and framing a waterfall spillway. We added spotlights overhead, and when it was finished, the whole basement pond glowed with a warm cedar-and-water look. It really did feel like a private spa.

The only hiccup was the waterfall filter. Its spillway wasn't deep enough to clear the wall's extra width, so it was delayed. Another lesson tucked away for later.

41 - *Finished upgraded indoor tank*

The Science: Lessons in Plumbing Genius

Joe's system was clever everywhere you looked. Every pipe had a union. Every filter and drain could be isolated with a knife valve. Repairs would be as simple as Lego blocks.

He even installed a Savio skimmer and a Savio filter, each with its own sewage drain for cleaning. An external pump circulated water from the settling tank through the filter and back into the pond. The return lines were hidden neatly under the cedar deck Eric would later finish.

By the time he was done, the plumbing wasn't just functional—it was beautiful.

The koi didn't care about unions or cedar cladding. They only cared that their water was clean and stable. But for us, the basement pond was proof we were finally learning to do things properly. Slowly, painfully, and with a lot of noise, we were becoming real pond builders.

LESSON: *Concrete takes months to cure depending on the location. It must cure slowly too, you cannot rush the process or it will crack. Don't rush the application of coatings.*

LESSON: *Spend money on box welded liners. The time you save is well worth the money spent.*

LESSON: *A skilled trades person is worth their weight in gold! DIYers love to do things themself. But sometimes, having a pro do the job gets it done better, faster, and cheaper.*

The Science: Concrete Chemistry vs. Pond Dreams

Concrete looks solid, but it's a living material for a long time after it's poured.

Fresh concrete is highly alkaline (pH 12–13). As it cures, lime leaches out, and the pH gradually drops. Until then, it can raise pond water high enough to harm or kill fish.

Concrete holds water like a sponge. Moisture stays locked inside the matrix • for months, slowly evaporating out. If you trap that moisture under a coating, it will bubble, peel, or flake off.

Curing takes patience. Industry standards recommend 28 days for structural curing, but ponds often need months before they're truly ready for coatings.

Why paint-on coatings can fail:

- They don't stick to damp surfaces.

- Escaping moisture forms blisters under the film.

- The high alkalinity can neutralize or chemically break down the coating itself.

What About Shotcrete?

Shotcrete (or Gunite) is concrete sprayed at high pressure onto a steel rebar frame. It's strong, versatile, and widely used in swimming pools. For ponds, it offers some benefits—and big caveats:

Pros:

- Fast application and sculpting of curves and shapes.

- Extremely strong when properly applied and reinforced.

- Can be waterproofed with a liner or high-quality pond-specific coating.

Cons:

- Requires structure. Shotcrete must be sprayed onto a steel rebar cage (or other structural frame). Without that skeleton, it will crack and collapse.

- Still alkaline, still porous—same curing and leaching issues as poured concrete.

- Prone to micro-cracks; any movement in soil or freeze-thaw cycles will open leaks.

- Requires expert application. A bad nozzleman = a bad pond.

- Always needs a waterproofing finish (liner, spray-on polyurea, or specialized sealer).For koi ponds, shotcrete is often overkill in cost and complexity. It works best for very large, formal designs where you want sculpted walls or integrated features. For most backyard ponds, a liner over a well-prepped base is more forgiving, cheaper, and easier to repair.

PRO TIP: *If you must use bare concrete, let it cure for at least three months, then acid-wash the surface to neutralize alkalinity before sealing.*

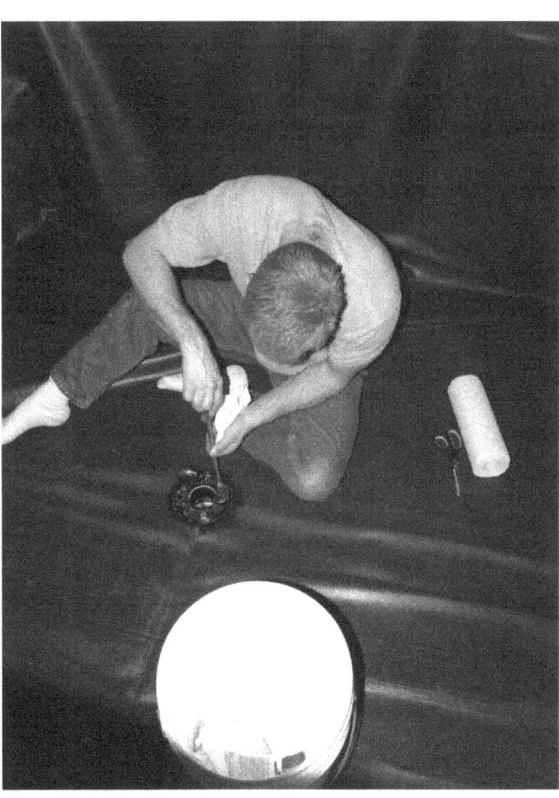

43 - *Joe installing bottom drain*

Sealers must be vapor-permeable—otherwise trapped moisture will push them off. When in doubt, choose an EPDM liner. Concrete always cracks eventually, and a liner is your insurance policy. With shotcrete, budget not just for the spray itself, but also the steel cage, rebar bending, and skilled nozzlemen—it's as much art as science.

44 - *Two return lines to create a current*

Fish Slide!

For some reason, November 17th has always been our drop-dead date for getting the pond covered for winter. Without fail, a miserable snowstorm hits around the 17th or 18th, plunging the temperature and making it nearly impossible—and dangerous—to move fish.

In 2007, we were facing that same deadline with a pond full of very large koi. By then, moving them was no small task—you can't carry big fish in your arms; you have to move them in water, which adds enormous weight. So I booked the help of two "fish guys" from Big Al's, a multinational pet store specializing in aquatics.

Building the Slide

The morning was cold, hovering around 41°F (5°C), and already edging toward freezing. The Big Al's team arrived at 8:00 a.m. and got to work pumping thousands of gallons of pond water into the basement tank. While the pump chugged away, they started building what they called a *fish slide.*

Out of 4×8 sheets of plywood, they rigged a ten-foot chute that fit neatly through the basement window and reached the edge of the indoor pond.

We lined it with leftover greenhouse plastic and slicked it down with a trickle of pumped water that came from the basement pond. It was simple, brilliant, and slippery enough for koi transport. By late morning, curious friends and neighbors gathered, doubling as "fish catchers" in case any overshot the pond and landed on the floor.

45 - *Fish slide ready to deploy*

The Fish Begin to Fly

The first few fish were easy to net, with the water dropped to hip depth. They tumbled down the slide, splashing into the basement pond—sideways in some cases—but always safely into the water. Soon we covered the pond with a green net, thanks to my friend Helder, to prevent the fish from leaping right back out.

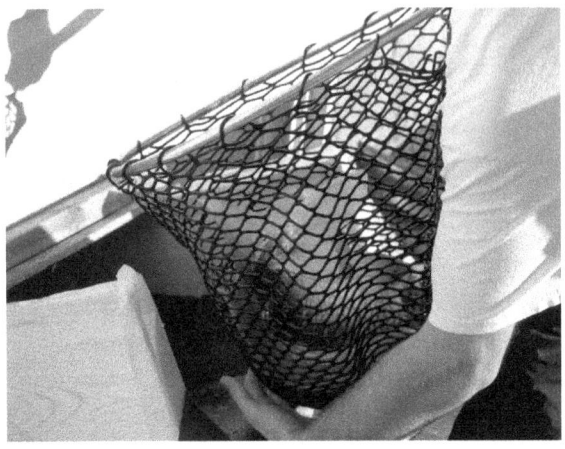

46 - There goes Caesar!

The weather turned harsher. Freezing rain stung the man in the outdoor pond, his fingers turning blue as he wrestled with the last, fastest koi. Hot chocolate helped a little, but in the end he had to drain the pond down to six inches to finally catch them. They slid through the chute, the basement window was closed, and the ordeal was over.

Inside, about eight of us stood around the pond—wet, tired, laughing, and passing around beers. The fish swam deep into their winter quarters, and I sat there thinking:

That was a lot of work, but I'm glad I didn't do it all myself. The fish slide had worked brilliantly.

Next spring, of course, I had no idea how we were going to get them back *out*. (It's not like there's a fish elevator! Or is there?)

PRO TIP: *Avoid New Pond Syndrome - Before moving the fish, bring one mature filter inside to seed the new pond.*

LESSON: *Sparkling clean water and brand-new filters look ready, but they are not biologically ready. It takes two to three months for nitrifying bacteria to colonize and reliably convert ammonia → nitrite → nitrate. During that time, fish are vulnerable.*

Spring Cleaning: A Word of Caution

New pond syndrome doesn't just strike new ponds. It also happens when you get a little too enthusiastic with spring cleaning. That brown, smelly gunk coating your filter media? It looks gross, but it's actually the workforce—your bacteria colonies doing the heavy lifting of detoxifying ammonia and nitrite.

Scrub it all away and congratulations: you've just fired your entire staff. The filter resets to Day 1, your water turns unstable, and your fish are left swimming in a toxic soup.

The rule: If it's alive, don't sterilize it. Rinse filter pads gently in pond water (never chlorinated tap water—that's napalm for bacteria). Leave some of the gunk behind. It's ugly, but it's saving your fish's lives.

And if your pond has rocks? Same rule. The brown gunk packed between those rocks is also part of the bio-army. Strip it all out and you're demolishing your bacteria's housing development. Better to let them keep their homes—and your fish will thank you for it.

The Science: New Pond Syndrome

Here's the un-funny part of ponding: filters don't work out of the box. They need to grow their own staff—little colonies of nitrifying bacteria—and those colonies don't show up overnight. This process is called cycling the filter, and if you ignore it, your fish will pay the price.

Think of it like this:

Day 1–3: You'll test and see nothing. Don't cheer—it doesn't mean your water is clean. It means your test kit is picking up zero activity.

Days 4–10: The first bacteria arrive and start eating ammonia. Suddenly your test shows: BAM! Ammonia spike. This is not a party. This is your fish swimming in poison.

Days 10–20: Ammonia begins to drop. Yay? Not quite. Because now the second bacteria show up, and they produce nitrite. Guess what? Nitrite is just as bad, and sometimes worse. Cue the nitrite spike.

Days 20–30 (and beyond): Slowly, nitrite falls as yet another bacterial team sets up shop, finally converting nitrite into nitrate. This is the milestone you're waiting for. Nitrate = your filter has officially "cycled."

And here's the kicker: even after you see nitrates, it takes another month or so before the system is robust enough to handle a full fish load without wobbling. Two to three months is normal. Anything faster means you got lucky (or you cheated with a mature filter).

To avoid disaster:

- **Seed filters**: Move in a mature filter, or cycle new ones with ammonium chloride and bottled bacteria before adding fish.

- **Feed lightly**: Above 15°C, once a day is plenty. Below that, don't feed at all. Hungry fish are better than dead fish.

- **Keep products handy**: Prime (or similar) for ammonia/nitrite, baking soda to stabilize carbonate, and ammonia detox to cover spikes.

48 - *Watching the fish come down the slide*

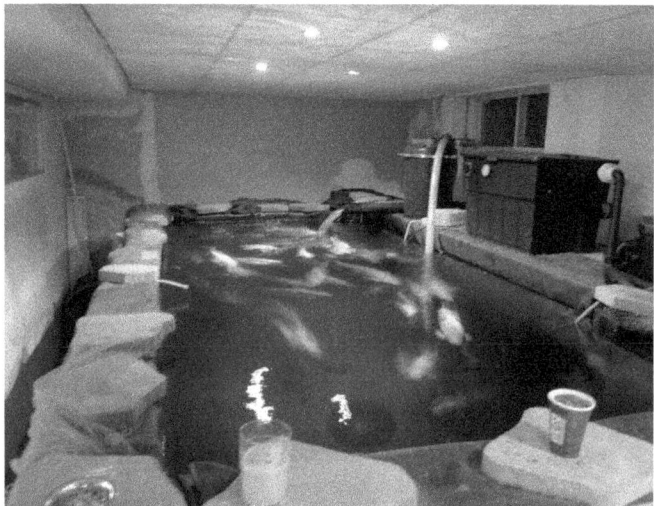

49 - *Everyone safe and sound in the new tank*

The Quiet Years

After the Great Fish Slide, life finally calmed down. We fell into a rhythm. The fish thrived in their indoor pond, and our new filter system worked beautifully.

Outside, the winter was as heavy as November 17th had promised. By spring, there was so much snowmelt that the pond had filled itself—free water, even better.

When we uncovered the pond and released the fish outside the following spring, they surprised us: not one of them tried to jump. And they made our 2,000-gallon pond look tiny. Nearly thirty big, graceful fish gliding around like they owned the place. They knew they were home.

50 - *"Dwarf" Papyrus plants in the corner*

That spring—2008—we finally got to decorate. We lined the edges with rocks we'd collected, and I invented hanging baskets using window boxes. I laid cedar fence boards across the pond's rim, weighted them down with stone, and hooked the boxes over them. It worked brilliantly: the plants thrived and the fish couldn't uproot them. I added whimsical garden art too—frogs, glass butterflies—to brighten up the dull siding of the house.

One of my favorite experiments was a dwarf papyrus. *"Dwarf,"* they said. By August, it was six feet tall and had a root ball the size of a laundry basket.

My daughter and her friend spent hours swimming in the pond that summer. In full sun, the water was warm and the fish loved the company.

That fall, the team from Big Al's wasn't available, so we moved the fish ourselves. No slide this time—just carefully carrying them, one by one, down the stairs. It worked. Another winter indoors passed safely.

I tried to overwinter the papyrus in our glass-surrounded bathroom. Huge mistake. Not only did it grow uncontrollably, it rotted, and the smell was… memorable. It was so heavy we couldn't remove it from the tub in one piece. So we split the root ball into a second laundry basket. It was very happy to be outside again, but we didn't overwinter it again.

By May 2009, the fish were outside again, happy in their big pond. We were really starting to live the pond life. Having living water on the property was magical—it drew birds, softened the climate, and kept our west-facing yard from becoming an oven in summer.

51 - *Koi doing well, grown to as much as 24" by 2010*

Spring 2010 brought another happy season, but we knew it would be the last time we carried the fish. They were simply too big now—Caesar was 24 inches long, and Miss Piggy and Amy weren't far behind. We couldn't keep hauling them ourselves or asking friends for help.

So I came up with a new cover plan: roof trusses. I hired a company to build and deliver them. They were huge—much larger than I expected. Our carpenter friend Eric helped us build a knee wall around the pond to stand them on. It took three people to carry each truss. Thankfully, my nephew Matt is tall and strong, and climbed across them like a trapeze artist, nailing everything in place. When we finished, it looked impressive—not quite a cathedral, but close.

Getting the plastic sheeting on wasn't hard, and the structure stood solid all winter. Jim never had to shovel it once. It even had a door and a boardwalk down the center, and on sunny days he'd go inside and just sit there, warm and peaceful under the plastic dome.

By spring 2011, the new cover had proven itself. Even our cats liked it, basking on the boardwalk in the early warmth. Plants sprouted under the cover by April, and by June the pond was overflowing with life. Water hyacinths covered half the surface and had to be thinned out.

Our filter system was fully mature now, having run non-stop for three and a half years between indoors and outdoors. No more New Pond Syndrome, no more emergencies—just balance.

At last, we could breathe.

There were no more problems. Just peace.

The pond had settled. The fish were thriving.

For a while, there was nothing to fix—only something beautiful to care for.

52 - *Nearly everything was perfect*

53 - *Looking down the inside of the truss cover 's walkway*

The Flood

I spoke too soon!

One summer, while my husband was out of town yet again (his timing is impeccable), a thunderstorm rolled in. At first it was just heavy rain—sheets of water pounding down—and I stood at the kitchen doors filming it. Then I noticed something odd. Water was pooling at the back fence instead of draining away.

Boots, raincoat, umbrella: I headed outside. Sure enough, four inches of water sat against the fence and was creeping up the yard toward the patio. Normally, it would disappear into the storm sewer connection on the other side of the fence, but not today.

Out front, what I saw stopped me cold. The street had turned into a lake, stretching across driveways and lawns for at least 50 meters. The water lapped over our curb. Every manhole up and down the block was spitting out water overwhelmed, their covers hidden beneath swirling vortices. The system was simply drowning.

54 - *The water covered the bottom 6" of the fence*

I dashed back to the pond. The water level had risen six inches. With no overflow built in, I worried it would spill over the walls. Thankfully, the skimmer was acting as an overflow. The trouble was, all that extra water was draining into the backyard, adding to the flood. Two-by-twelves we had leaned against the fence were floating like unmanned ships, and the stone path around the willow vanished beneath water. The "lake" was marching toward the gardens.

I had to stop the pond from feeding it. I grabbed a spare submersible pump, every hose and length of pipe I could cobble together, and strung a line toward the front yard. Balancing bricks over the cord so it wouldn't fall into the pond, I crouched in the wind and rain, trying not to electrocute myself as I plugged it in. Success—the pump roared to life! Except I hadn't connected the hose.

Cursing, I scrambled back, attached it, and then chased leaks as I shoved one dripping pipe into another until water finally poured onto the driveway. Crude, but it worked.

Back in the shed, things weren't much better. My two settling tanks were floating like barrels in a flooded basement. The water inside wasn't heavy enough to hold them down, so I hauled patio stones on top of them to keep the plumbing from tearing itself apart.

55 - *The water had reached the gardens, now about 12" deep*

The storm didn't let up for another hour. The pond was still overflowing through the skimmer, the pump was barely keeping pace with the rainfall, and the backyard flood crept higher. By then, water at the fence was a foot deep.

That's when Jim's taxi pulled up. He stepped out, dry and composed from his flight, only to find me soaked and wild-eyed, standing in two inches of water. He looked at me, raised an eyebrow, and said, "You look like a drowned rat. What happened?"

I gestured at the street-turned-lake. "I've been battling Mother Nature for two hours. Nice of you to ask." He finally noticed the flood swallowing our neighborhood, turned back just as the taxi vanished around the corner, and muttered an "oh my God."

When he saw the backyard, his reaction was less polite. By then I had the pump jury-rigged with hopes and prayers, and I warned him not to touch it. If he fiddled, the whole thing might collapse.

We spent the rest of the evening monitoring the water, hoping it wouldn't rise any higher—because the last thing you want is groundwater mixing with pond water. Runoff carries who-knows-what: pesticides, insecticides, poisoned rodents. It's a toxic soup you never want to dump on your koi.

Finally, the rain slowed, the sewers caught up, and the ground began to drain. The water drained away, leaving only mud, debris, and a valuable lesson.

LESSON: *Always build your pond edge higher than ground level. Mother Nature doesn't ask permission, and groundwater is not welcome in a koi. Planning ahead for excess water can mean the difference between a soggy yard and a disaster for your fish.*

The Science: When Floodwaters Rise—Pond Keeper's Checklist

Floods don't just threaten your basement—they can overwhelm your pond in minutes. Even if your fish survive the rising water, the contaminants that come with it may not spare them.

Why floodwater is dangerous:

Chemical contamination: Runoff may carry fertilizers, pesticides, road salt, or toxins from neighboring yards.

Pathogens: Standing water can introduce parasites, bacteria, or viruses.

Oxygen depletion: Mud and organic debris decompose, consuming oxygen rapidly.

Structural stress: Rising water can float filters, shift plumbing, or undermine pond edges.

If you live in a flood-prone area:

- Build pond edges higher than surrounding ground to keep surface runoff out.
- Install an intentional overflow line or skimmer outlet directed away from the pond area.
- Keep a spare submersible pump and hose ready to move water fast.
- Store heavy objects (like patio stones) nearby to weigh down floating barrels or tanks.
- Keep all electrical connections elevated and protected from standing water.

You can't control the weather, but you can control how ready you are. A little preparation means your pond survives the storm alongside you.

The Science: Be Ready for Power Outages

Ponds depend on pumps and filters to stay alive—literally.

If the power goes out, oxygen levels can crash fast especially in warm weather.

That's why we invested in two tri-fuel generators (they can run on natural gas, propane, or gasoline) to keep everything running. It might sound over-the-top, but when you've spent years raising koi, you do what it takes to protect them.

Here's what we've learned:

- **Size it right**. Add up the starting watts (not just running watts) of your pumps, air blowers, and filter motors—this information is usually online—then add about 25% extra for safety.

- **Alternate units**. Generators can't run forever. They need a break to cool down, so we have two identical models and rotate them during long outages.

- **Stock supplies**. Keep spare fuel and motor oil on hand, and store them safely.

- **Rehearse it**. Run a test drill. Figure out which heavy-duty three-prong extension cords reach where you need them, and practice switching things over—so when the power fails at 2 a.m., you'll already know what to do.

- **Maintain it**. Check your generator's manual for how often to run it for upkeep, and follow the maintenance schedule religiously.

It might feel like over-preparing—until the night the lights go out and your pond keeps humming along while the rest of the neighborhood goes dark.

Recommended Tri-Fuel Generators

56 - *Firman Tri-Fuel 5000 watts*

57 - *Generac Portable Generator 8,000 watts*

The Science: Storm & Flood Preparedness for Pond Owners

Severe storms and flooding are becoming more common—and ponds are vulnerable. Here's how to prepare before the skies open up:

Before the Storm

☐ Raise the edges: Ensure your pond walls or berms are higher than the surrounding grade. Add temporary sandbags if flooding is predicted.

☐ Secure equipment: Anchor filter barrels, UV units, and pumps so they can't float or tip.

☐ Protect power: Elevate electrical connections, use weatherproof covers, and unplug non-essential gear.

☐ Pre-pump: Lower the pond water level a few inches ahead of heavy rain so it can take on stormwater without overflowing.

☐ Emergency pump & hose: Keep a spare submersible pump and long hose ready to move water away from the pond.

☐ Netting or covers: If high winds are forecast, secure netting or a cover to prevent debris from being blown in.

☐ Have a generator available and ready to go. (It's easier to deploy in a storm if it's already in place!)

During the Storm

☐ Don't wade into floodwater with live electrical cords—safety first.

☐ Focus on keeping an open overflow path so the pond doesn't breach its edges.

After the Storm

☐ Test water immediately (ammonia, nitrite, KH, pH).

☐ Watch for contaminants: if you suspect runoff, do partial water changes gradually.

☐ Add extra aeration—debris decomposition consumes oxygen fast.

☐ Observe fish closely for stress, flashing, or clamped fins.

☐ Keep dechlorinator and salt on hand in case you need emergency treatment.

58 - The flood water had filled up our yard and everyone else's entirely

The Truss Years

As I mentioned already, our fish had grown so large, they were very difficult to transport up stairs. Some were well over 24" long. Even with the help of family and friends, it became a dangerous task carrying a large, heavy fish in water up a flight of stairs, across the house and into the backyard.

We decided to leave them outside again, but this time I would come up with a different way to cover the pond. Something safer than the dome, stronger, and able to survive winter storms.

The answer came one day when I saw an advertisement for a company that made garage roof trusses on TV.

Eric the carpenter set up a "knee wall" all the way around the pond that would support the trusses. We used strapping lengthwise to hold them all steady and stable and then covered them with greenhouse plastic. The plastic was kept in place with strapping running the vertically. It was the most stable structure we ever had and we used and reused those trusses for three years. Even storing the trusses wasn't that much of a problem, as they neatly stacked in the garage.

59 - *Trusses installed on top of a knee wall*

The truss years, as I like to call them, were good years. The pond flourished. The plants thrived. We upgraded our filters bit by bit, learning as we went.

Fighting "Green" Water

Green water is everyone's problem. It's pervasive, and hard to conquer. What you need to understand, is that green water is "natural". It is the result of sunlight, water, and food. If you compare other bodies of water like oceans and lakes, you notice they too have green water—for the most part.

Rivers are the exception. Why? Because the water is *always* moving.

60 - Early days – shading the pond with a tarp

Our pond was green from day one. I hated it. Couldn't see the fish, and I knew it was causing other problems—but I didn't quite understand what was happening. We tried every solution out there: Barley straw, peroxide, and algaecide.

At one point we installed an industrial-sized UV light with six bulbs, hoping to rid ourselves of green water. It worked… somewhat. Unfortunately, the UV bulbs were only good for one year. With six of them, it was too expensive to keep using – something we didn't know when we purchased it. The unit kept the algae lessened, but not 100% gone. If it had worked completely, it would have been worth the cost.

LESSON: *Scale everything to fit how many gallons you have in your pond. A 20,000 pond needs equipment that can handle 20,000 gallons. That seems a silly statement, but you'd be surprised how frequently that rule is disrespected.*

How does UV Work?

Ultraviolet light "bursts" the single cell algae plants, killing them. But UV *only* works when the flow rate of the water through the UV unit is slow enough for the UV to kill the algae. That meant it had to flow more slowly through the UV than it did through the filter. One UV unit wasn't enough to clarify 20,000 gallons of water and still keep up with the full sun in our back yard. We would have needed several of those units all flowing together, putting through a minimum of 50% of the water every hour.

If all our algae experiments taught me one thing, it was this: *the only true cure for algae is shade*.

Everything else only slows it down. When we tried algaecide—it made the fish sick. We even tried dyeing the water blue—it only made the fish disappear.

Our only real success was *shade*.

The Science: How UV Clarifiers Work and How to Size Them

Pond UV units serve two different goals:

•   Clarification (green-water algae control): Deliver enough UV dose to disrupt single-celled algae so they clump and get removed by filters.

•   Sterilization (pathogens): Much higher UV dose to inactivate bacteria/parasites. Most koi keepers are aiming for clarification, not full sterilization.

The physics in one line:

UV dose = intensity × exposure time.

If water flies past the lamps too quickly, exposure time drops and the dose falls below the level needed to keep water clear.

Practical Targets (Rules of Thumb)

Dose needed (typical):

•   Clarification: ~30 mJ/cm² (30,000 µW·s/cm²)

•   Sterilization: ~90+ mJ/cm² (often 90–180 mJ/cm²)

Wattage planning for clarification: ~10–15 W per 1,000 gallons as a starting point if flow and UV-transmittance are good. Heavier sunlight/nutrients or murkier water will need more.

Flow through UV for clarification: Often 1/4 to 1/3 of total system turnover routed through UV at a moderate pace, not the full pump blast. Use a bypass manifold to tune flow across the UV chamber.

Why Flow Rate Matters

•   Too fast: algae survive the pass → haze/green tint persists.

•   Too slow: you don't process enough pond volume per hour to "keep up" with growth; water can heat around the lamps; efficiency drops.

Sweet spot: a steady, moderate flow where each pass gets an adequate dose, and the whole pond volume still cycles through UV frequently enough to hold clarity.

The Science: The Truth About Algae

Algae are simple aquatic plants that thrive on sunlight, nutrients, and warm, still water—and every pond has them.

Here's what most people get wrong:

Shade, Not Plants, Stops Algae

"If you have plants, you won't get algae."—Myth

Plants don't prevent algae; they only compete for nutrients. Even a lush pond will grow algae if sunlight reaches the bottom. The only reliable long-term control is shade—from floating plants, tall marginals, or tree cover that blocks sunlight from hitting the water.

Algae Cause Daily pH Swings

Algae can swing wildly in algae-heavy ponds. By day, algae remove CO_2, which raises pH (more alkaline). By night, they release CO_2, forming carbonic acid and lowering pH (more acidic). This constant up-and-down stresses fish, even if the average pH looks "normal" on a single test.

They Steal Oxygen at Night

During the day, algae make oxygen. At night, they consume it—competing directly with your fish. Heavy algae growth can cause oxygen crashes just before dawn, when dissolved oxygen is lowest and fish are most vulnerable.

Gimmicks Don't Solve It

Barley straw, UV lights, chemical algaecides, and blue dyes only offer temporary or partial results—and may harm fish if misused. Shade is the only lasting solution. Once you take away the light, the algae can't win.

If you don't want algae, don't FEED it sunlight!

When the Wind Has Teeth

As our big maple tree grew tall enough to cast afternoon shadows across the pond, the algae began to retreat. We tried to help it along with tarps, but they never stayed put—not in the windstorms Ottawa is famous for.

There's something about the way our neighborhood is laid out.

The wind comes howling over our roof, whips straight down behind the house, and slams into the pond like a wall. I don't know the physics, but it's destructive.

We used to have a hexagonal metal gazebo on the patio. One summer afternoon, the wind came howling. You can always tell when it's coming—first the tops of the forest trees sway one way, then the linden tree by the house starts swaying the other. Then the howl hits.

That day, Jim and I were doing yard work in the front. The howl came with a crash so loud I bolted to the back door.

I stopped dead. The gazebo… was gone. "Jim, the gazebo's gone!" I yelled.

"What do you mean gone?" He skidded to a stop beside me, eyes wide at the empty yard. The chairs were toppled, the cat fence torn, and the gazebo had simply… vanished.

"Where's the gazebo?"

"I don't know!"

Jim ran upstairs, then called down: "It's next door! Upside down and crumpled like a dead spider."

We stood gaping. It had sailed clean over a seven-foot fence, without hitting a single thing.

The neighbors weren't home, so Jim quietly let himself into their yard and retrieved the wreckage, piece by twisted piece. There was no saving it. We gave it up for scrap and bought a new one.

The second gazebo, we tied down like a stubborn dog—to rings on the fence posts and a screw tie-out in the ground. It never flew again.

It took us years (and a flying gazebo) to figure it out. We normally experience easterly winds—coming from the west blowing toward the east. But every now and then they turn and come back the other direction—from the east—and hit our house head on.

Here's what's happening:

- As strong winds crest our roof, they accelerate, spill over the far side, they slam down into our backyard, creating sudden *turbulent downdrafts*.

- This air turbulence hits like a wall—flattening plants, stressing fish, and trying to rip anything light or flat into the sky.

- That's how our hexagonal gazebo was lifted clean over a 7-foot fence without touching a thing and what caused the loud booming of the dome. You could literally see those domes being pushed down like an invisible hand was there. (A very large hand)

LESSON: *If the wind can get under it, it can take it. Anchor everything light and flat—tarps, pond covers, gazebos—like they're trying to escape… because they are.*

The Science: About Wind Hazards

If your house is creating wind problems, this is what's happening:

Your house and roof line are creating **wind shear** and **Bernoulli*** effects

The strong west winds flow up and over your roof, which **accelerates the air as it crests the roof line**.

When that fast air hits the sheltered space behind your house (your yard), it **suddenly drops in pressure and speed**

This creates **turbulence, downdrafts, and vortex eddies** that slam straight down into your backyard—like invisible hammer blows

Flat or hollow structures (tarps, gazebos, pond covers) give the wind something to "grab", and when the wind gets under them, *it lifts them like sails*—even tossing your gazebo over a 7-foot fence!

In short: your yard is a ***wind trap***—it's where the fast, high-pressure air spills and crashes.

*The Bernoulli effect describes the principle that in a moving fluid (liquid or gas), an increase in speed occurs with a simultaneous decrease in pressure.

While a great system, let's face it, wooden roof trusses are not meant to be carried around, assembled and disassembled every year. They're heavy and awkward to maneuver. It takes three people to move one, and getting them around corners and through fences?

After three years of wrestling the truss pieces every spring and fall, and calling in every favour we could, there were no more people to help up us with the trusses. In the spring of 2013, when we took the cover apart for the last time I sold them to a man who was building a garage. He was delighted, and so was I at not having to store them in the garage again!

That autumn, for the first time, we left the fish outside without a cover.

That proved to be another mistake.

61 - *Truss cover in winter*

62 - Truss cover seen from the back of the yard

The Anomaly Year

When you look up Ottawa's weather during the winter of 2013 on Google, this is what you get:

> *"The winter of 2013 for Ottawa included a significant warm spell in late January, with a day reaching +12°C (53.6°F), and a long cold spell from February 1–11. While Ottawa is generally known for cold winters and snowfall, the 2013 winter was marked by these specific temperature extremes within the typical colder-than-average periods."* ... *Google Search AI Overview*

What that doesn't capture is just how bizarre it really was.

It got cold by mid-November, as usual. By the end of the month, there was a thick layer of ice on the pond. December buried us in snow—so much that its weight collapsed the snow crust down by twelve inches.

Then January arrived like spring with temperatures in the 50sF (10+C).

The roller coaster was dizzying. Warm spells, deep freezes, then warm again.

Why That Matters for Fish

Fish don't cope well with wide temperature swings and they were outside without a cover that winter.

Water is slow to warm, but quick to cool. It can take weeks of sunshine to bring it up even a few degrees, and only a couple of cold nights to send the temperature plummeting.

63 - November had lots of snow

By January 30, after weeks of warmth, the pond was melting. Open water gleamed, and the fish had risen toward the top.

Two days later, the temperature plunged to –18°F (–28 °C), a 70-degree drop Fahrenheit (30C) in 36 hours—and stayed there for over a week.

The pond refroze quickly, trapping the fish near the surface. Then it thawed again. Then froze again.

And all the while, the water level was mysteriously dropping—eight inches in just a few days. There was nothing we could do until spring.

The Empty Pond

When spring finally came, the damage was plain: We lost them all. Every single fish.

We decided to use the tragedy as an opportunity.

With no one left to keep alive, we did a full clean-out—drained everything, scrubbed the EPDM liner, and sanitized the red algae bloom with Hydrogen peroxide.

We checked every connection for leaks; even 64 - *A pond without fish*
lifted the deck boards and dug down to the pipes.
We didn't find any leaks. So, we filled the pond again and restarted the filters.

With no fish to produce ammonia, I jump-started the cycle with ammonium chloride and bottled bacteria. We added floating plants.

Then we just… watched the water.

One day, I turned to Jim and asked, "Why are we doing this?"

"What?"

"Running an empty pond?"

"It's pretty. I like the water."

"It's a lot of money for just water. Maybe we should fill it in. Losing them all was really hard."

"Find out what it would cost."

The Cost of Giving Up

I did. And it was shocking. I called a local landscaping company and they helped me calculate what I would need in terms of material, how much, and what types. To create a stable surface would need to use hundreds of cubic feet of crushed stone in different layers, and then top it off with soil and finally grass.

Here are the numbers:

- 1,920 cu ft of stone/fill—$6,000
- Remove debris and rock—$1,000
- 3 yards of topsoil—$2,000
- Sod—$2,000
- Deconstruct shed, fill and remove debris—$5,000
        Total: $16,000.

To have… flat grass and nothing else. That just seemed pointless.

We could sell off the equipment, but it felt like going backward. We looked at each other. No. We'd start over. But this time, the fish would come inside for the winter.

The New Six

The very next weekend, we drove to Clarke Koi in Toronto and bought five sizeable koi. No babies this time. We wanted presence, not a restart from scratch.

The trip home took five hours. By the time we arrived we were already worried about the fish. When I opened the boxes in the back yard, the smell of *Melafix* hit me. Melafix is a product made by API that is used to treat bacterial infections. It has an anesthetic affect, so is good for keeping fish calm during transport. It helps keep the fish from feeling too much stress. However, this was way too strong. The fish were gulping at the surface, listless and weak.

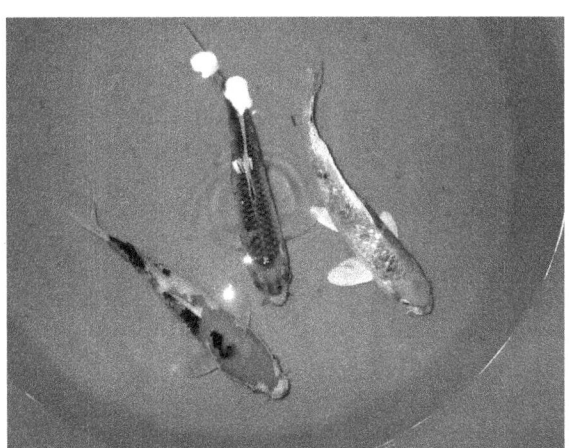

65 - *A Sanke, Sushui, and a Gin Rin Hariwake*

I couldn't leave them in that soup to "acclimatize." So we grabbed some totes, and I opened their bags and placed them in the totes, with a couple of buckets of pond water to dilute the Melafix and an air stone. They struggled so I cradled each fish until they were breathing, then placed them into the pond by hand. One hung motionless.

"Come on, little one, breathe."

A gulp, then his gills moved… and he darted down to the bottom.

The next revived slower. The third never revived at all.

I was heartbroken—again.

We got the remaining survivors into the pond. They huddled at the bottom in a single square metre of space. I phoned Clarke Koi, and they were upset as well. They suspected too much Melafix had been used. They offered to replace the lost fish.

By bus. Yes—by *Greyhound Bus Lines*.

A week later, we waited at the bus station like expectant parents. The bus was late. Our poor fish.

At the bus station, I frantically kept checking the arrival time of the bus. It was delayed and we didn't know why. Jim kept standing at the ticket desk bothering them every few minutes until we got a reason: traffic. Finally, the bus pulled into the station and we rushed out to speak to the driver and retrieve the box marked "LIVE FISH". We didn't do the same thing this trip, we had a tote ready with an air stone and clean water in the car. We opened the box immediately, and place the fish in the tote. We plugged the air pump into the car, and started the drive home.

This time the ride wasn't as harrowing and the fish arrived in good condition. When they joined their friends at the bottom the whole group schooled and got the tour of the pond.

Six fish. Down from thirty.

Beginning Again

In time, they recovered. They began exploring the whole pond, and finally came to the surface for food. They thrived that summer—all six of them.

When autumn came, we prepped the indoor tank. It was a simple job this time. Just six fish to catch.

The Science: How to Safely Add New Fish

Koi are sensitive to temperature shock and pathogens, so introducing them to your pond carefully is crucial—especially if your pond is already established.

Here's the safe method:

- **Float the bag**: Place the sealed transport bag in your pond (or better, a quarantine tank) for 15–20 minutes to let the temperatures equalize.

- **Add a little pond water**: Open the bag and add small amounts of pond water every few minutes for another 10–15 minutes to help them adjust to your pond's water chemistry.

- **Move fish, not water**: Gently lift the fish out of the bag with clean hands or a soft net and place them into the pond. Do not pour the transport water into your pond—it may contain waste or medications (like Melafix) that could harm your system.
- **Quarantine**: If you have an established pond, always place new fish in a quarantine tank for 2–4 weeks first. This prevents introducing parasites or disease to your main pond.
- **Slow acclimation:** To avoid shock—give the fish 20 minutes to adjust to your pond's ecosystem safe.

PRO TIP: *Don't add the bag water with the fish. The water you transport your fish in is highly toxic and low in oxygen. Just move the fish—not the water.*

Transport water is usually high in ammonia and low in dissolved oxygen. It can also contain waste, stress hormones, or medications. So don't add it to your pond. Pouring it into your pond can damage your water quality or harm your biofilter. And you never know what is in the water in terms of microscopic problems.

The Science: Why Temperature Swings Kill Fish

Koi are cold-hardy fish—but only if the temperature changes slowly.
They don't die from cold alone. They die from shock.
Here's what happens:

- Cold slows their bodies: As water cools gradually, koi go dormant, sinking to the bottom and slowing their metabolism.
- Warm spells wake them up: Sudden warmth makes them swim to the top and start using energy reserves—but their immune systems are still shut down.
- Cold crashes hit like a hammer: When temperatures plunge again, they're caught at the surface, still active, and now burning energy they can't replace.

- Repeated freeze–thaw cycles are deadly: This yo-yo pattern leads to exhaustion, organ failure, and often death—especially when oxygen is low under ice.

LESSON: *A stable cold is safer than a swinging one. Consistent winter temperatures let koi stay fully dormant until spring.*

Normally, new fish should slowly be acclimated to your pond's temperature and pH. This is done by floating the bag in which you brought them home, in the pond for about 20 minutes while slowly adding a little pond water to the bag. Then your fish won't be shocked.

Sometimes that's not possible—like when they're in distress.

PRO TIP: *In an emergency—like transport water contaminated with too much Melafix—get them into clean, oxygenated pond water fast. Try to match the temperature of the water if you can. Cold or heat shock is damaging.*

A good pond cover helps buffer against sudden weather changes. It keeps warm spells from waking the fish—and keeps cold snaps from shocking them.

The Leak and the Leap

The Vanishing Pond

The fish had overwintered beautifully during the 2014–2015 season. By early March, though, a massive snowfall brought a surprise: the sheer weight of the snow collapsed the ice cover on the pond, and the whole frozen sheet plunged down into the water below.

That's when we discovered something was very wrong.

The water level was nearly twenty inches below where the ice had formed. By the time all that snow finished melting—probably late April—the pond was only half full. Given how much snow had fallen, I'd expected it to be brimming. Instead, it sat stubbornly low.

The Science: How Tiny Leaks Drain Huge Ponds

Water is relentless. Even a pinhole leak in an EPDM liner can drain a pond shockingly fast.

A simple way to understand this:

Imagine turning a tap so it's just barely dripping—maybe one drop per second.

That seems like nothing… until you leave on it overnight. By morning, you'll have more than 2 litres (½ gallon) of water in the bucket.

Now scale that up to a pond, where the water behind that pinhole is under hydrostatic pressure from thousands of gallons pushing outward. That pressure forces water through the hole faster than gravity alone would allow. What looks like "just a tiny puncture" can empty a pond by a foot or more in a single night.

Suspecting a leak, Jim and I began our detective work. The trick to finding a leak is to wait until the water stops dropping. Wherever it stops, the hole is just above that waterline—maybe only by a quarter of an inch. But spotting a hole in EPDM is maddening. It only takes a pinprick to drain a pond.

The Science: Finding a Leak by Waterline

Leaks are notoriously hard to find, but there's one key trick: Water stops dropping once it's below the level of the leak.

As water drains, it will keep falling until the hole is exposed to air. Once the leak is no longer submerged, it can't pull water through anymore.

This is why the best time to look for a leak is when the water level has stopped falling—you know the hole is just above that line, often only a few millimeters higher. It still takes sharp eyes (or a diver in scuba gear, in our case), but this method narrows down the search zone dramatically.

LESSON: *Small holes are big problems. Always secure bulkheads in concrete, and double-seal liner penetrations.*

We delayed moving the fish back outside. Jim suited up in scuba gear to search underwater while I filled the pond right to the brim, then monitored how fast it dropped. At first it took a week to lose a foot. By June, it was losing that much *overnight*. We were refilling it daily—so much that the City of Ottawa called to ask if our plumbing had exploded. When we explained about the leak, they verbally shrugged and said, "You'll still have to pay for it." Our summer water bill was atrocious.

Eventually, with the pond nearly empty again, we found the culprit: the rubber liner had pulled away around the bulkhead where the return pipe passed through. The hole was huge, gushing water. Worse, the force had scoured the sandbags behind the liner. The sand hadn't vanished, exactly, but water had washed it out of the bags, leaving hollow voids behind. The water pressure pushed the liner backward until it broke the seal entirely.

Never rely on sand. Not even in bags. It shifts, washes away, and undermines everything UNLESS you reinforce it with concrete behind the liner to prevent movement.

And yes—fifteen years earlier, some "expert" had dumped thirty tons of sand into the hole. I'd had my doubts even then.

So 2015 was a write-off. The fish stayed in the basement. The pond outside sat empty, awaiting its fate.

Chipmunk Invasion Sidebar

Meanwhile, life at our house is never dull, even without a working pond. One day, one of our young cats marched proudly into the kitchen and deposited a very live chipmunk on the floor. Then he walked away.

The chipmunk froze, wide-eyed. Realizing he was probably about to die, he bolted under the stove. With the cats prowling and no safe way to grab him, we concocted a ridiculous but brilliant plan: the Chipmunk Tunnel.

We uncoiled about forty feet of 4-inch collapsible drain pipe—the accordion kind with slots used in French drains—stretching it across the kitchen floor, through the patio door, and out into the grass. We blocked every other escape route from under the stove and waited. A few hours later, while we watched TV, we heard tiny claws scrabbling through the pipe. He shot out into the backyard like a furry cannonball. Mission accomplished.

It wasn't our only rescue. Another time, while airing out the house, I watched a short-tailed chipmunk dash straight down the hallway, chittering happily, before the cats noticed him. He hid behind a bookcase. We set up the pipe tunnel again, and eventually he took it. A week later, the same chipmunk came back—but this time strutted right out the front door, pausing to glare at me as if to say, "I'll do it my way."

To this day, chipmunks live under our deck, in the woodpile, and even in the garage. One chewed a perfect one-and-a-half-inch doorway through the garage door frame just for himself. When we built a new deck behind the pond, they moved in immediately. I'm certain the deck near the house will have its own thriving chipmunk colony by winter. They're part of the household now.

Rethinking Everything

By the end of that summer, we faced a big decision: solve the problem or give up. Since we're not the kind of people who give up easily, we chose to find a solution. We could lay a new liner over the old one; but the same issue might happen again unless we rebuilt the wall behind it. Or we could start over entirely.

Fate gave us a nudge. We received a small windfall from a family member's estate, enough to do things properly. So we decided: no more patching. No more oversized, unmanageable pond. We would build a new, final pond the right way.

Designing the Dream Pond

I spent months drawing plans and consulting fish breeders and equipment specialists. The first decision was to reduce the size. Yeah, everyone dreams of a "bigger pond", but sometimes it can be too big for your budget. So, instead of 20,000 gallons, we scaled down to a deep but smaller formal rectangle of about 9,500 gallons—plenty for our six koi, easier to maintain, and far less overwhelming.

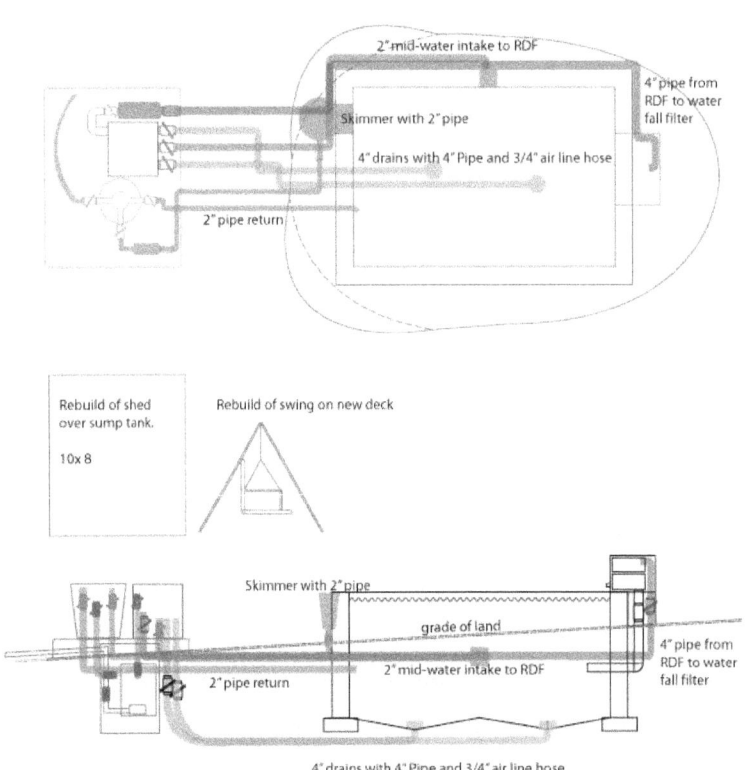

68 - *My concept of the new pond*

This time, I wanted strength and insulation. The new tank would be built with Insulated Concrete Forms (ICF)—interlocking foam blocks with rebar inside, stacked like Lego, then filled with six inches of poured concrete.

The new filtration system became my obsession. I designed it around:

- A *Zakki Shower*, biofilter—custom-built by Zak of **Deep Water Koi** in Florida. He used ceramic cylinders in horizontal trays inside a Schedule 40 PVC box frame.

- A *ProfiDrum*, designed in Germany, but sold by Mike Swanson of **Koi Acres** in the US, to remove solids.

- Two *ClearGuard 16000*, pressure filters from **Danner Manufacturing**, for polishing and supplemental biofiltration.

- A *Helix Skimmer*, by the **PondDigger** in California—a fish-safe design that lets curious koi swim back out unharmed.

- Two *aerated bottom drains* with dome diffusers designed by **Koi Acres** to keep oxygenated water circulating.

- *Knife-edge waterfall* box to provide sound.

- A *Whole-home Centaur Charcoal* water filter from **Aquatel**.

- Two return locations to create a current; one mid-water and one deep water.

All the QR Codes for these suppliers are listed at the end of this chapter for your convenience.

Sizing the pumps was tricky—Canada measures in litres per hour, and the numbers look deceptively high. I needed real power: about 9,000 gallons per hour to feed the shower, with additional flow from the bottom drains and mid-water return. Between gravity feeds and suction, we planned for over 13,000 gallons per hour through the system.

For the first time, I was genuinely excited about the technical side. This pond would be efficient, balanced, and beautiful.

69 - *The Koi Kastle*

Life in the Basement

Meanwhile, the fish remained indoors for another year—and needed enrichment. One day, we spotted a plastic discarded above-ground pool staircase on the curb. My brother and Jim saw a castle.

They cut huge arches into the sides, front, and back to make swim-through tunnels. We christened it the Koi Kastle and lugged it downstairs. I grabbed my camera as they heaved it into the water… where it promptly floated like a giant cork and drifted into the center of the tank. We weighed it down with concrete pavers.

Within days, the koi were exploring. Within a week, they were hiding under it constantly and refusing to swim anywhere else. That wasn't quite the intended enrichment. We pulled it out and left it at the end of the driveway with a "Free" sign.

Preparing for the Big Build

By December, I had found a contractor experienced in ICF construction. All that remained was to prep the site—remove the rocks, demolish the old shed, and clear space for the backhoe.

It was going to be a very busy summer…but for the first time in years, it finally felt like we were building something that would last.

The Science: How to Find a Leak in EPDM liner

Finding a liner leak takes patience, but there's a reliable method:

Stop refilling. Let the pond water drop naturally—no pumps running, just still water.

Wait for the waterline to stop falling. This is the key clue. When the water stops dropping, the leak is just above the surface.

Mark the level. Use a grease pencil or tape on the liner or rocks to show exactly where the water stopped.

Inspect the perimeter at that level. Slowly walk the whole edge, pressing gently on the liner. Look for: damp soil just beyond the liner, tiny tears, pinholes, or cracks spots where fittings or bulkheads go through the wall

If the hole's underwater, drain lower. If you suspect it's deeper, lower the water another few inches and watch for where the line stops again.

PRO TIP: *Wear polarized sunglasses on a sunny day—they cut surface glare and make it easier to see tiny damage in the liner.*

71 - Looking for leaks … in all the wrong places

QR Links

77 - Danner Mfg

72 - Deep Water Koi

76 - Helix Skimmers

73 - Koi Acres

75 - Aquatel

74 - ProfiDrum

79 - *Zakki Shower* biofilter

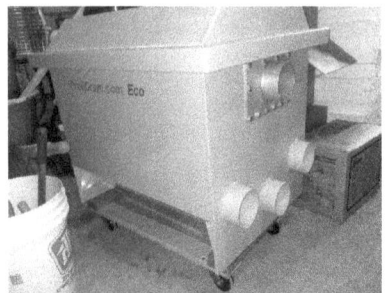

78 - *ProfiDrum* rotary drum filter

81 - *Helix fish safe skimmer*

82 - *Teton EcoStream pump*

80 - *ClearGuard 16000*

The Summer of Ruin and Renewal (2016)

The Great Backyard Emptying

We had one summer—and that means barely two months—to completely clear out our backyard. That may not sound like much, but our yard is big. And soon, there would be a backhoe tearing it all up.

The goal: dismantle everything.

The old pond, its plumbing, rocks, plants, shed, decorations—all of it had to go, right down to bare ground, so we could prep the site for new construction. The liner had a hole in it and was unsalvageable. It felt wasteful to throw away such a massive piece of EPDM liner, but at least we'd never paid for it—it had been a gift from the company.

Ironically, the original contractor who had dug the hole back in 2002 showed up, asking if we still had the liner he'd installed. I told him no—but he was welcome to the one we were pulling out. He happily took it.

83 - Moving and sorting rocks

Sand, Stone, and Sorrow

Once the liner and underlayment came out, we could see the skeleton of the old build: hundreds of sandbags stacked like bricks around the walls. To our surprise, with the exception of those behind the leak, they were all intact. None had burst, none had leaked, and none had shifted in fourteen years. They were actually excellent at encasing sand—as long as they never got wet. Sand is permeable, meaning water goes through it.

The Science: Sandbags and Water: How They Actually Behave

Sandbags are designed to be permeable.

Standard sandbags (the kind recommended by the U.S. Army Corps of Engineers and used worldwide in flood control) are made of woven polypropylene or burlap. They are meant to let water slowly seep through rather than block it entirely.

Why this is good in floods:

Their purpose is weight and slowing water, not sealing it out. The sand absorbs water, becomes heavy, and the bags knit together into a semi-solid barrier that slows flow and redirects water. They work because they stack fast and resist erosion—but they don't create a watertight wall.

Why it can be bad in ponds:

If you have a leak in the pond liner, this will soak the sand in the bags behind it. This leads to the sand being washed away, forming a void behind the liner.

This makes the liner vulnerable to being punctured, or a hole forming if the void is behind a connection.

In flood use:

Sandbag walls are always considered temporary. After floods recede, they are removed because they rot, burst, or leach their contents if left sitting in water. They're never meant as permanent structural material.

So in short: the army recommended them because they're quick, cheap, and disposable—perfect for emergency flood barriers, but completely unsuited to long-term underwater use like pond walls. But with a liner in front of them, they form a perfectly stable wall – as long as there are NO leaks.

We left them in place, because the new tank would be smaller—about 16 by 10 feet—and would sit inside the old hole. But everything else had to come out.

The rocks were the worst.

Our friend Pierce came over to help Jim move the boulders, and even with a dolly they could only manage a few at a time. It took them several weekends just to clear the big ones and stack them on the driveway. We dismantled the old waterfall and pulled out the tank hidden underneath, along with the jagged "dragon's tooth" rock we'd once been so proud of.

Then came the river rock: three different sizes wrapped around the pond like a stony beach—four to five inch cobbles, one to two inch stones, and finally the fine pea gravel sprinkled on top. Jim and I sorted them all by size, laying them out on tarps across the lawn. We knew the grass was doomed, but the backyard was now a construction zone and we had nowhere else to put them.

After the rocks came the liner. Jim climbed into the drained pond with a utility knife, slicing the massive sheet into strips we could actually carry. We rolled the strips up like black carpet and stacked them on the driveway.

Pulling the liner off the back wall was heartbreaking. It revealed the true extent of the damage: the bulkhead that had leaked had shifted as the ground slowly moved over the years. Any pipe penetrating a pond wall must be locked into concrete, we learned—because the earth always moves. Even a tiny shift can break the tight seal a bulkhead depends on.

Free to a Good Home

Once the worst of the mess was cleared, I posted on social media:

> *"Free landscaping rocks of all sizes. Bring gloves and a wheelbarrow."*

84 - Bags exposed and damage found

Within hours, a man messaged me. He was building a rock garden and would take all we could give. Over several days, he and his son worked tirelessly, hauling away every boulder, every river stone, every last bit of gravel. It saved him a fortune—and it saved us from hauling it ourselves.

I did the same with the old equipment we weren't keeping: the skimmer, waterfall tank, bits of pipe. Piece by piece, it all found new homes.

Taking Down the Shed

By then the backyard was starting to look barren—no pond, no rocks, no garden. Just a raw scar of earth. The shed still had to go.

Pierce came back, this time with my nephew Matthew, and the two of them cheerfully demolished it. To be fair, it was basically a fence in a square, but it still took effort. We left the old foundation of concrete block in place; removing it would have been far too much work, and we figured the new shed could simply be built around it.

At the time, I even considered lining that old block box with EPDM to turn it into a settling tank—but the new ProfiDrum made that idea unnecessary.

A Backyard Laid Bare

When the last of the rocks were gone, the liner removed, the shed torn down, and the plants cleared away, I stood looking at what remained.

It wasn't a pond anymore. It wasn't even a garden.

It was just a sandy crater rimmed with ancient sandbags—a hollow, desolate pit surrounded by mud and torn-up lawn. My once-beautiful backyard was gone. The serenity, the sound of running water, the peaceful green world I'd built—gone.

I stood there at the edge of the wreckage, exhausted and filthy, and quietly cried.

And I whispered to myself, Oh, God… please let this all be worth it.

85 - *Everything dismantled. What have we wrought?*

Building the Dream (2017)

Stockpiling the Plumbing

By early spring of 2017, everything was ready.

The fish were safe and healthy in the basement. The old pond had been completely dismantled. We had salvaged what we could, given away what we didn't need, and the backyard was nothing but bare earth waiting for its transformation.

Months earlier, I'd done what any determined ponder does: I ordered every piece of specialty plumbing I believed I needed. The heart of the system would be 4-inch schedule 40 PVC—fittings, unions, sleeves, and valves that weren't available anywhere in Canada at the time. I sourced them all from one US supplier, shipped them to a border depot, and Jim and I drove down to collect them.

That turned out to be its own adventure.

It was the first year of Donald Trump's presidency, and there was a strange new tension at the border. Coming back, the guards were abrupt and suspicious. I walked in to declare the boxes properly, receipt in hand, and quoted the value from memory—in US dollars—while holding the actual receipt to show them.

Big mistake.

Suddenly I was being accused of trying to smuggle plumbing supplies. They wanted to search the car. My attempts to explain (which have never helped anything) only made it worse, until Jim quietly elbowed me to stop talking. (Not the first time ☺) Eventually they relented, and we limped back across the border with all our boxes intact—and my dignity slightly dented.

Those boxes sat stacked on our patio, hundreds of fittings and lengths of pipe gleaming like treasure. They were my insurance policy. With those parts, I knew I could build the plumbing system of my dreams—or fix it if something went wrong.

Breaking Ground

The contractor was supposed to start in April, but the spring of 2017 brought record-breaking rain. It poured for weeks, and he fell behind on other jobs. At last, he promised to break ground in mid-June.

The backhoe rumbled into our backyard on June 12. I stood at the window, heart hammering. After years of planning, sketches, spreadsheets, and false starts… it was finally happening.

86 - *TaggerWear my business was moving out*

And just to keep life interesting, this was also the exact moment we were moving my business out of the house and into our new factory. The lease began on Canada Day, July 1, and movers were already packing up our workrooms.

So while heavy machinery tore up our backyard, other crews were dismantling our business around us.

It added a surreal kind of stress—juggling equipment lists, contractors, freight schedules, and floor plans at the same time as arguing about pond footings. Every day felt like a high-stakes plate-spinning act.

The first thing the contractor asked was whether we had blueprints. I proudly showed him my detailed, scaled drawings—layout, dimensions, elevations, plumbing lines, electrical runs, the works.

He glanced at them and said, "That's not good enough."

He wanted formal stamped blueprints.

So I found an architectural engineer who specialized in oddball projects, and $1,200 later, I handed the contractor a beautiful set of blueprints. They specified everything:

- the exact siting of the pond aligned with the house windows

- the shed position

- the plumbing and electrical lines

- and the crucial elevations: *six and a half feet in the ground and eighteen inches above.*

87 - Dug in the wrong place

That wall height was important to me—it was tall enough to make the pond deep and safe for over-wintering the koi, but also a perfect sitting height around the edge.

I also gave him my plumbing schematics, which showed every line:

- the twin 4" bottom drains leading to the shed

- the mid-water return

- the 2" deep-water return

- the skimmer-to-shed run

- and the return to the future knife-edge waterfall.

In theory, everything was perfectly planned.

In practice, nothing went the way it was supposed to. As usual.

Cracks in the Foundation

Instead of building inside the footprint of the old pond as we'd specified, the backhoe tore down the entire side wall and squared the hole off. Mounds of dirt and sandbags towered along the fence, as tall as the fence itself. The backyard looked like a battlefield.

88 - Dumped in the middle of the pond!

Then they framed the footings—and I immediately saw they were wrong.

They didn't look six and a half feet down. I got a tape measure and checked. From ground level to the top of the footing was barely fifty inches.

I called the contractor inside and laid the blueprints on the kitchen table.

"This isn't right," I said. "The footings are too shallow. And they're not even in the right place."

His response? "I didn't bother following the blueprint."

I stared at him. "Then why did you make me spend $1,200 on it?"

109

89 - *Boom truck for the concrete*

He scowled, muttered, and left in a huff—but the next day his crew dug the footings deeper, about another 12–14 inches. Unfortunately, they piled all the soil into the center of the pond basin, exactly where the bottom drain trench was supposed to go.

When I pointed this out, he got angry again. "Not my fault. We're just doing what you told us."

"I did not tell you to dump it in the middle of the pond," I replied.

More muttering. More huffing.

They waited until the footings were poured and the first ICF blocks were in place. Then he sent two teenage laborers, who spent the entire day groaning about the heat, the dirt, and their life choices while very slowly clearing the soil out of the middle. But at least it got done.

The Street Spectacle

Then came the big show: the cement truck and the boom truck.

The boom's arm stretched over the house like a giant mechanical crane, pouring concrete into the footings while neighbors gathered to watch. Our street was chaos—trucks, workers, spectators—and as if on cue, our neighbor was installing a massive preformed fiberglass swimming pool the same day. A semi arrived with the pool shell while a crane lifted it over his house.

It was like a backyard construction festival.

Our footings cured while his pool filled.

The Lego Walls

When the contractor returned, they began building the walls from Insulated Concrete Forms (ICF). It was fascinating to watch: giant foam Lego blocks locked together, with rebar running through their centers.

And then the weather struck again.

A week of torrential rain turned the clay soil to soup. On the side where they excavated the soil and bags, the clay dirt was exposed and once saturated collapsed inward, knocking into the uncured walls and toppling part of it. The crew had to dig out the

90 - *Rain-soaked clay collapse*

91 - *Boom operator filling walls*

mess, stabilize the slope, and rebuild before continuing. The other side, where there were still bags, did not collapse.

Once the walls were complete, they pushed pipe sleeves through the foam for the future plumbing lines. Then the boom truck returned, and they poured concrete into the hollow ICF blocks. Skilled workers poked long rebar rods down into the wet concrete to release trapped air bubbles. Finally, they left the structure to cure for two weeks.

Agile technicians ran along scaffolding, controlling the business end of the boom truck where the cement was pouring out like a tap. The hose roared and pulsed as the concrete surged through it, the pump thumping in time like a distant drum.

The Science: Concrete Doesn't Dry—It Cures

People often talk about concrete "drying," but that's not what's happening.

Concrete is a mix of cement, sand, gravel, and water. The water triggers a chemical reaction called hydration. As the cement hydrates, it bonds the sand and gravel together into a solid mass.

If concrete dries out too soon, this reaction stops—leaving it weak and crumbly. That's why concrete is often misted or covered during its early curing stage: it needs moisture to harden properly.

Concrete also comes in different strengths, measured in MPa (megapascals). Most garden structures use 20–25 MPa. For pond walls, you want at least 30 MPa, since water pressure will be pushing on them constantly.

> *LESSON:* *Concrete hardens by curing, not drying—and stronger mixes are essential for pond walls.*

The smell of wet cement rose on the damp air—sharp, earthy, and cold. The hollow blocks trembled slightly under the workers' boots as they danced along the edges, perfectly balanced, guiding the heavy hose with effortless precision. It was quite the sight—and proof of just how sturdy those blocks already were.

The Science: How insulated concrete forms (ICF) Work

Insulated Concrete Forms (ICF) are like giant Lego blocks made of high-density foam. Each block has two thick foam panels connected by plastic webs. Workers stack them up like toy bricks, reinforcing them with rebar as they go, and then fill the hollow center with concrete.

Now a common building material in house-building, they provided a double insulated wall, effective in cold climates for keeping heat in, and cold out.

Once cured, you get a sandwich wall:

> 4" of foam on the inside
>
> 6" of solid reinforced concrete in the center
>
> 4" of foam on the outside

The foam stays in place permanently, giving you excellent insulation and structural strength. For a pond, that means warmer water in winter, cooler water in summer, and a tank strong enough to resist the pressure of thousands of gallons.

> *LESSON:* *ICF walls are energy-efficient, structurally strong, and perfect for building deep, insulated ponds.*

The Fresh Water Fiasco

One of the side projects we'd had their so-called plumber do was install a Centaur Whole Home charcoal filter in the house. It was a fantastic decision—it strips out chlorine, chloramine, and other toxins before the water even enters the house. Our water has been delicious ever since.

From there, we asked them to run a fresh water supply line outside to the future filter shed.

Inside, the work was fine—functional, if messy and uninspired. Outside was another story.

LESSON: *Catalytic carbon neutralizes hidden toxins that harm fish, protects your biofilters, and makes your water smell and taste wonderfully clean.*

The Science: How Catalytic Carbon Protects Your Fish

Tap water is treated with disinfectants to keep it safe for humans—mainly Chlorine and Chloramine. These chemicals kill bacteria... but they also burn delicate fish gills, damage slime coats, and disrupt beneficial pond bacteria. Even tiny amounts are toxic to koi.

Centaur Catalytic Carbon is a unique type of granular activated carbon (GAC) made through a patented catalytic process. This process gives the carbon a specially treated surface that accelerates chemical reactions, so it doesn't just absorb contaminants—it breaks them down.

It's particularly effective at removing:

- Chloramine, a chlorine-ammonia molecule (NH_2Cl), which standard carbon struggles with
- Hydrogen sulphide, the gas responsible for that "rotten egg" smell in some water supplies

By installing this filter on your home's main water line, every drop of water entering your house—and your pond—is free of these dangerous compounds.

LESSON: *If your city uses chloramine, you need catalytic carbon (ochemical water conditioners) to fully neutralize it—and keep your koi safe.*

93 - *Water pipe must be buried 8ft*

They buried the fresh water pipe a mere **18 inches below grade**. In Ottawa, our frost line goes down about four feet.

I knew immediately this was wrong. A shallow line would freeze solid in winter and could burst, flooding our yard—and worse, it could backflow into our house plumbing. So I fought them on it.

Luckily, I knew a guy who worked for the city in the department that sets these regulations and handles inspections. He very kindly gave me a letter on letterhead stating the actual law: **fresh water supply lines anywhere in Ottawa must be buried eight feet down**. Otherwise, the installer could be held liable for flooding damages.

Ooooh, that got their attention.

I stayed home for this one. They had to dig up the line, drill it properly through our basement wall at eight feet down, and rebury it the full length of the yard—all the way under the future shed foundation wall.

This time, at least, they did it right.

But it shouldn't have taken a legal threat to make them do their job.

The Science: Why chloramine replaced chlorine

For decades, municipal water systems disinfected drinking water with chlorine. Chlorine is powerful but volatile—it evaporates out quickly once the water reaches your tap. That's great for fishkeepers, because it can be removed easily with simple carbon filtration or by letting water sit to off-gas.

But there's a problem: chlorine doesn't last long in the miles of pipes that carry water across a city.

To solve this, many cities switched to chloramine, a compound made by combining chlorine with ammonia. Chloramine is much more stable, staying active all the way from the treatment plant to your tap. That protects people—but creates new headaches for pond keepers.

Here's why:

- Chloramine doesn't evaporate like chlorine does
- Standard carbon filters only remove the chlorine part, leaving behind toxic ammonia
- Ammonia fuels algae blooms and burns fish gills

LESSON: *Always bury water supply lines below your local frost depth—or be ready for ice, ruptures, and lawsuits.*

The Science: Why Water Lines Must Be Below Frost Line

Water expands when it freezes—and it expands with astonishing force.

If water inside a pipe freezes, it creates pressure that can split the pipe wide open, sending cracks along its length or even blowing out fittings entirely. When it thaws, all that hidden damage becomes a flood.

In places like Ottawa, the ground can freeze down to about four feet during winter. This depth is called the frost line or frost depth. Any water-carrying pipe that sits above that line is at risk of freezing solid.

To protect against this, building code requires:

- Fresh water supply lines to be buried at least 8 feet down, well below the frost line
- Drain pipes can often be shallower, because they're dry most of the time
- Burying the pipe deeply keeps it in soil that stays above freezing all winter, and it also protects it from shifting or heaving as the soil freezes and thaws.

The Plumbing Disaster

While the walls cured, the contractor's plumber installed the bottom drain lines.

94 - *Drains connected with 90° elbows*

When I came home that day and looked down into the pit, my heart sank.

Instead of running each line straight off the drain, he made three ninety degree turns before leaving the tank. Three sharp corners on a line meant to carry fish waste—the heaviest, dirtiest water in the whole system.

Even amateur pond keepers know you keep waste lines straight. You don't use 90° elbows in plumbing unless it's absolutely unavoidable—you use sweeps (long 90s) to keep the flow smooth. Where on earth had this plumber learned his trade?

I didn't have the time—or the brain space—to babysit this crew!

I had hired professionals because I believed they would do the job properly, to spec, without me needing to hover. Little did I know the contractor wasn't supervising either. No one was supervising. And no one was following the blueprints.

Every day, we'd come home from the factory—where we were installing machines, setting up equipment, and moving our entire business into the new building—only to find some new disaster at the pond site. Every. Single. Day.

Most of it I let go. The improper placement. The wrong depths, even after they'd been corrected once. Because I had to pick my battles.

But this mistake was a show-stopper. I confronted the contractor. He folded his arms.

"I'm not redoing it."

"You have to. It won't work."

"It'll work fine. I've done things for you I wouldn't normally do. I'm not doing this."

That was the moment I'd had enough.

"You're fired," I said. "Do not bring your crew back here. And you're not getting another dime."

The Science: Why 90° Bends Are Bad for Waste Lines

The contractor's plumber installed three sharp 90° elbows on the 4-inch bottom drain lines. That's a mistake you don't need to be a plumber to recognize.

Waste lines are meant to carry the heaviest, dirtiest water in the pond—full of fish solids. To move that water, you need straight, smooth runs so gravity can do its work. Every sharp 90° corner becomes a trap where solids collect, slowing the flow and eventually clogging the line.

The correct way to turn a corner is to use a sweep (also called a long 90). A sweep has a long, gentle radius that lets water flow through without breaking momentum. It takes more planning to lay out a sweep—they eat up more space—but it's the only way to keep waste lines clear.

Avoid sharp elbows on bottom drain plumbing. Use sweeps, and keep the runs as straight as possible.

Choosing Not to Fight

We'd already paid him $17,000.

We consulted a lawyer, but it would have to go through small claims court, where we'd have to represent ourselves. Even if we won, no one would enforce the payment. We could spend months fighting and still never see a cent.

So we walked away. We'd been here before: betrayed by a contractor, left with a half-done mess. We knew what came next. We'd fix it ourselves again.

I called Joe, our trusted plumber, and sent him photos of the mangled drain lines.

"Good grief," he said (though not in those exact words). "We can't leave it like that."

"I know," I said.

"But I'm booked solid this summer. I can't get to it until next year."

"Then it will wait until next year."

A Hollow Victory

Before they left, the contractor's crew backfilled the pond walls and buried every inch of their work. Conveniently, we couldn't see any of it anymore.

Somewhere under the soil was a disaster waiting to happen.

Our backyard would become an archaeological dig next year.

But at least the walls were standing.

At least we still had our dream—and the mountain of fittings stacked on the deck, right?

The Vanishing PVC

After I they left, we began picking up what we could of the disaster site—trying to take stock of what was left.

That's when I opened the boxes of schedule 40 PVC fittings I had so carefully ordered and brought back from United States.

They were almost all *empty*.

At first, I thought they'd stolen them—taken the most expensive parts for resale. It would have made sense. That was even part of what we considered including in a possible lawsuit.

But as we started piecing together what had happened, we realized the truth: **they hadn't stolen the fittings**. *They'd used them. All of them. Underground.*

No plan. No map. No record.

Everything I'd sourced and stockpiled was now buried under our yard in a mystery labyrinth of unknown plumbing. It was almost worse than theft. If they'd stolen them, at least they'd be gone.

Now they were hidden land mines under our feet.

The Mouse Water Park

By the time Joe finally came to help, we already knew something was wrong.

We'd seen the tops of the pipes poking up like periscopes from the ground. There were too many of them. And they weren't where they were supposed to be.

So we began to dig.

95 - *Digging out the buried pipes*

At first, it felt like a normal job—just clearing away a bit of soil to expose the buried PVC runs. But the deeper we went, the stranger it became. Pipes snaked everywhere, looping under each other, twisting like drunken spaghetti. Elbows were glued end-to-end like beads on a necklace. Tees sprouted sideways into nowhere, capped off mid-run like forgotten branches. Some fittings weren't even glued—just dry-fitted and buried like they'd given up halfway through.

By day two, the "system" looked less like plumbing and more like the skeleton of a roller coaster for mice.

We started calling it the archaeological dig. We took photos from every angle. We needed proof—because no one would believe this without seeing it. When we finally showed the montage to a few commercial plumbers, one of them took one look, raised his eyebrows, and said,

"That's not plumbing. That's a mouse waterpark."

We couldn't have described it better.

It was funny—until it wasn't.

Every sharp 90° turn was a trap for fish waste. Every flat run was a sludge collector. Every buried joint was a future leak. This was supposed to be the backbone of our filtration system, and instead it was a catastrophe waiting to happen.

119

Joe just stared at it all, shook his head slowly, and muttered, "The more I dig up, the more problems I find." Then after a long pause: "I would fire this person if he worked for me. This is beyond bad work."

It took us months. Nearly the entire summer.

Weekends spent on our hands and knees with shovels and cutters, unearthing and salvaging what we could. Joe saved as much straight pipe as possible, but most of the fittings were toast—cut off, tossed aside, and eventually recycled. It was painful to see almost $4000 worth of brand-new go into the garbage bin.

I think I laughed. The kind of laugh you do when your brain can't decide whether to cry or start screaming.

By the time we were done, the ground around the shed looked like a bomb site.

96 - Mousepark, Part 1

97 - Mousepark, Part 2

But at least the "Mouse Waterpark" was gone—and we could finally start building the system the *right* way.

Pond Archeology 101

Rebuilding from the Ground Up

We disconnected the bottom drains, straightened them, and ran new pipes cleanly down the center of the pond, sloping gently up to emerge in the shed.

We salvaged the straight sections, but most of the elbows had to go—heartbreaking when 4" fittings cost $30–$50 each.

With the drains redone, we built a concrete block foundation wall around the shed site. Joe reinstalled the 4" return lines, which had been set at strange angles, and we dug all the way to the footing to get at them.

Eventually, the standpipes stood neatly in their proper places. Pierce came back to rebury them and grade the ground. There was far too much dirt—they'd removed mountains for no reason—so we were left with hills where there should have been flat, and hollows where there shouldn't.

But by fall, it almost looked like a backyard again.

Liner, Shed, and Systems

We kept the styrofoam panels covered with tarps until they were buried, then regrouped the next spring to install a new EPDM liner.

98 - *Salvaged pipes, installed properly!*

That's when I discovered my rookie mistake: I had forgotten stairs. There was no way in or out of the tank without a ladder.

99 - *New shed built by a plumber!*

We folded the liner into hospital corners, smoothed the wrinkles with water, drained it, then Joe sealed all the bulkheads—two 4" returns at one end, a 2" return at the other, a mid-water intake, and two 4" bottom drains. We refilled slowly, checking for tension or twists.

Meanwhile, Joe volunteered to build our filter shed. His carpentry was immaculate—full plywood cladding inside and out, fully insulated, built like a house so we could mount heavy equipment directly to the walls. He even built a floating floor over the pit under the shed and included two trap doors for access to store things like pipe and fittings.

We had an electrician install a pony panel for 45 amps of power, light switches, outlets, and a garage-style heater to keep the shed just above freezing in winter.

And yes—an air conditioner. It sounds excessive, but it keeps humidity from wrecking the pumps. It doesn't run much, but it keeps the tiny building dry and stable.

Pandemic Pause

Then COVID-19 hit.

Everything stopped.

Our business ground to a halt. The only thing that saved us from going under was a sudden order to print custom fabric surgical masks through our sewing business.

Jim spent the first lockdown shingling the shed roof and installing the siding by himself.

100 - *ProfiDrum being installed*

By May, Joe was back, working alone inside the shed. He mounted the ProfiDrum on an adjustable pump stand to match the pond's water level, and set the shower filter on a raised shelf to keep the floor clear.

By June, everything was connected. Joe filled all the pipes and left them for weeks to test for leaks. No water loss. No leaks.

The rest of the year was eerily quiet. No pond work. No youth sports. No factory running.

Jim and I spent hours downstairs, watching the fish—the only calm in a world that had come apart at the seams.

In a way, we were lucky. Being a writer, Jim could work from home.

And we had our fish.

The Science: Water Runs Downhill

Drain Slopes and Gravity Flow

Bottom drains rely on gravity-fed flow. This only works when pipes slope steadily downhill toward the filter system. Any rise or dip in the line creates settlement zones where waste collects, clogs form, and anaerobic bacteria thrive.

The ideal slope is about 1–2% (1–2 cm/m or 1in/yd) for gravity drains.

Static Head Pressure

The height of the water column (pond water level vs. filter system level) creates static head pressure. If the system is not levelled properly, pumps must work harder to overcome that pressure, wasting energy and reducing lifespan.

The Science: Why Straight is Best for Pipework

Friction Loss and Flow Resistance

Every elbow, joint, and unnecessary bend creates turbulence and friction loss in water flow. In smooth, straight runs, water stays mostly laminar (smooth layers). But each sharp turn breaks that laminar flow into turbulent flow, which increases resistance dramatically.

A single 90° elbow in PVC pipe adds as much resistance as several feet of straight pipe.

Three elbows in a row? You're basically halving the flow rate—and overworking your pump.

Siphon and Air Locks

Pipes that dip down and back up create trapped air pockets. These act like "speed bumps" in your plumbing. They can also trigger siphon effects (uncontrolled flow when water suddenly starts moving downhill), which is dangerous in pond systems because it can drain water unexpectedly during power outages.

Anchoring and Thermal Movement

Unsupported PVC can shift, sag, and flex as temperatures change. This can cause:

- Stress at joints
- Microfractures in glued fittings
- Gradual loosening that leads to leaks years later
- Anchoring lines prevents that "roller coaster" effect you found.

The Science: Ensuring a Good Seal

Why EPDM liner Works

EPDM (Ethylene Propylene Diene Monomer) is a synthetic rubber that stays flexible in temperatures from -40°F (-40°C) to 248°F (120°C). It's:

- UV-stable (won't crack in sunlight)
- Inert (won't leach toxins)
- Elastic (stretches and shifts with soil movement)

Bulkhead Seals and Liner Stress

Installing bulkheads through a liner requires stress relief—folds must be smoothed so no tension pulls on the seal. Any torque or twisting can cause creep failure, where the rubber stretches and eventually tears around the fitting.

A typical drain installation has a two part bulkhead.

1. Under the liner, the pipe is either welded or threaded to the bulkhead,
2. Silicone is applied on top of the bulkhead plate (use only fish-safe silicone),
3. The liner is on top of that,
4. Next is another layer of silicone, then the gasket and another layer of silicon,
5. The top half of the bulkhead goes top of the gasket,
6. Screws go through all layers. Then the aerating dome sits on top.

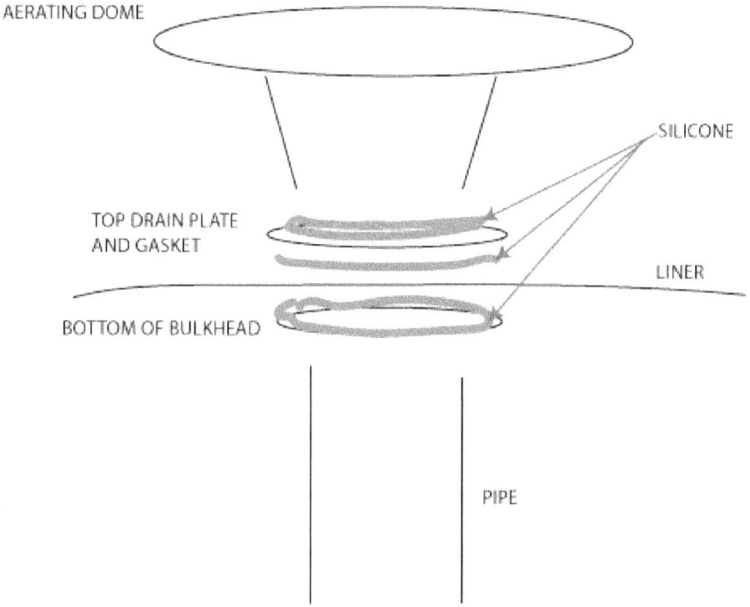

AERATING DOME

SILICONE

TOP DRAIN PLATE
AND GASKET

LINER

BOTTOM OF BULKHEAD

PIPE

101 - *Typical drain installation in liner*

The Science: Using the Right Sealant

Why silicone is your friend—and how to use it right

A watertight bulkhead depends on two things:

- No stress on the EPDM liner (no tension, twisting, or folds pulling on it), and
- A flexible, permanent sealant that bonds to both the liner and the fitting.

This is where silicone sealant comes in—and not just any kind. I must be fish-friendly.

Why Silicone Works

Silicone stays elastic, even after it cures. Unlike rigid adhesives, it can stretch and move with the liner as temperatures change or the ground shifts. That keeps the seal from cracking or peeling loose. It's also waterproof, inert, and non-toxic once cured—safe for fish, and stable in both freezing and high-heat conditions.

Not All Silicone Is Created Equal

There are three main types you'll see on the shelf:

1. Acetoxy-cure silicone
   - Smells like vinegar while curing
   - Cures quickly, but can corrode metals (especially aluminum)
   - Generally not rated for constant water immersion

2. Neutral-cure silicone
   - Odourless, safe on metals and plastics, and bonds to EPDM liner
   - Slightly slower cure time
   - Best choice for pond use

3. Aquarium or Marine silicone – this is the one you want.
   - A type of neutral-cure silicone
   - Specifically designed for constant submersion, and fish-safe
   - Some brands you can find include: ASI Clear Aquarium Silicone, Aquascape Black Silicone, and Marineland Silicone.

PRO TIP: *Always check the label for "neutral cure" and "safe for aquatic use". If it doesn't say it, don't use it.*

The Science: How to Apply Sealant Correctly

1. Make sure the liner and fitting surfaces are clean, dry, and free of oils or dust.

2. Apply a thin, even bead around the fitting where it presses to the liner.

3. Tighten the bulkhead firmly—but not enough to squeeze all the silicone out.

4. Wipe away excess and allow 24–48 hours to cure before filling the pond.

Done right, that seal can last decades.

Where to Use Silicone:
- Bulkheads – between layers, on outside and inside.
- Drains – under the liner between the bulkhead and lining, on top between lining and gasket, and between drain and gasket.

Don't Use Construction Adhesives

Products like PL Premium and other polyurethane-based construction adhesives <u>do not belong anywhere near your EPDM</u> liner or bulkhead fittings.

They're strong—but they're also:

- **Rigid when cured** → they crack as the liner flexes

- **Not rated for constant water contact** → they soften and fail over time

- **Potentially toxic to fish** → solvents can leach into the water

- They might seem like a quick fix, but they won't stay watertight.

- Worse, removing them later usually means cutting the liner—and no one wants to do that.

Bottom line: Stick with neutral-cure, aquarium-safe silicone. It stays flexible, seals beautifully, and plays nicely with rubber, plastic, and fish.

The Long Calm

Opening: Return to Water

We waited a full four seasons before the fish went home. Why? To test the new pond under all conditions first, and to give the new filters time to fully cycle and mature. We didn't want new pond syndrome.

It was a triumphant return. In 2022, the fish were brought back outside for the last time. Oh boy, were they big. Eight years in the basement, with year-round feeding, had made them grow and grow. Most of them were nearly full grown and a minimum of 30" in length. They were heavy!

But when they were put into the new pond, it looked right. They were able to swim deep and jump without fear. Even though the footprint of the tank inside was nearly the same as the one outside, the added depth and width made all the difference.

But getting here took four years of trial and error. Errors we made in judgment, errors from assumptions, and just plain forgetting things. The kind of situation any of us can find ourselves in.

The TojaGrid Gazebo

As soon as the fish were in the pond, the first question came to mind: what about winter?

The previous year, we had just covered the pond with a flat cover, but that didn't prevent the water from freezing on the top. Along came a company called TojaGrid—a Canadian company that had designed an easy way to build pergolas.

I fell in love with the look of them immediately, and ordered a kit the size of our pond. Originally, I had planned on building a gazebo over the pond by hand. To that end, there were post saddles embedded in the corners of the pond walls, and in the middle of the long walls.

103 - TojaGrid.ca

129

With TojaGrid, all we needed to do was attach their post feet to the wall. The best thing about this product was that it was assembled in a few hours by four of us. The tricky part was getting it over the pond. Normally people are putting them over patios… not us. We're special. We have to do it the hard way—over ponds.

104 - *TojaGrid structure over pond with shades*

Once up, it served as the perfect frame for our pond dome. (More on that later.) We're so happy with Toja that we purchased another kit to make a pergola over the newly installed patio this past summer (2025).

The first winter, I devised a frame for the dome that used the TojaGrid structure as its support. I built a wooden box around the legs and attached the PVC hoops to this box using pipe brackets. The plastic sheet was then laid over the hoops and clamped to the frame with wooden blocks to hold it under tension, which compressed it firmly in place. The ends were folded in neatly and secured the same way—with blocks holding the plastic in place.

On one end, my husband built a doorway he hung from the TojaGrid structure, allowing him to "get inside" the dome if necessary. The second year, we got rid of the doorway and simply go under the plastic.

That dome worked like a charm. No shoveling, no unzipping, no collapsing. We've reused that same structure for the past three winters—with a few minor changes to reduce the work. Now we can cover the pond in one day.

Our future plans for the pond gazebo include a permanent rigid clear cover on the top of the structure, either in Polycarbonate or similar material like Lexan. Then we would have side and end panels that could be installed for the winter and easily stored during the summer.

The Deep Water Return Redesign

The first thing we discovered during the pressure test was that we couldn't push the water from the ClearGuard pressure filter and have it make it all the way to the furthest end of the pond. The distance was simply too great.

I thought I understood the physics… nope.

I reread the instructions for the filter (something I hadn't done in years) and realized my mistake: the filter was designed to have a *short run* between it and the waterfall. Short, as in not 25 feet across and 8 feet down.

Joe had to get creative, because nothing was going to be relocated—the waterfall would stay where it was, the filter would stay where it was, and the pipes weren't moving.

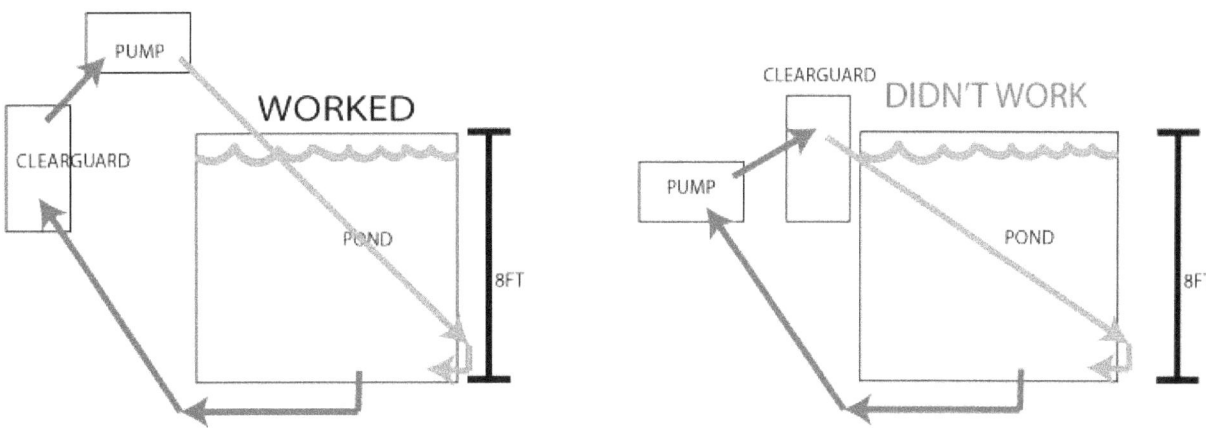

105 - *Pump configuration for deep water return*

We had one gift: the ClearGuard was capable of pushing 8,000 gph, and the PVC pipe was capable of handling about 4,000–5,000 gph pressure. We realized the pump couldn't stay on the inlet side of the filter as it normally would. It looked strange, but it worked—beautifully.

Joe wondered: what about *pulling* the water through the filter?

There was nothing in the instructions that said we couldn't. Even Danner, the filter's manufacturer, didn't know if it would work. Joe—the ever elastic-thinking plumber—changed the configuration so the pump was above the filter, pulling water *through* the filter and then pushing it down the return pipe. It was now *after* the filter.

After he got all the air out, flooded the pump, and filled the filter with water, it worked beautifully. To make sure it would always start on its own after a power failure, he installed a one-way valve to stop the pipes from draining, a bleeder valve at the top of the pipe stack, and a way to flood the pump manually if all else failed.

It has worked flawlessly ever since, even through repeated power outages.

This was all about head pressure—the resistance created by distance and elevation. The further and deeper water must travel, the harder the pump must push, and the more pressure builds inside the filter housing.

The Science: Pump-Filter Order is Important for Deep Water

What happened when the pump was before filter and deep water return

(Pump → ClearGuard → 25 ft → return 10 ft down)

- The pump pushed water into the ClearGuard, which is a pressure filter.

- This created high head pressure inside the filter housing.
- The pump had to overcome both the internal resistance of the filter + the weight of the water column going 25 ft and 10 ft down.
- Because the outlet pointed down, any tiny air pocket in the filter would rise back toward the pump and break prime.
- The ClearGuard was never fully flooded under pressure—it became a "closed bubble" resisting flow.

Result: The pump stalled out, cavitated (air causes turbulence), and lost prime.

ClearGuard → Pump → 25 ft → 10 ft down

- Now the filter flooded passively by gravity from the pond before the pump even turned on.
- The pump sucked through a full filter and pushed water downhill—something centrifugal pumps excel at.
- The outlet pipe stayed full of water because the vertical drop created a siphon effect, and gravity helped keep it primed.

Result: No air, no pressure buildup in the filter, smooth startup every time.

The Key Principle

- A flooded filter feeding a flooded pump is happy—the pump pushes water effortlessly.
- A pressurized filter resisting a pump builds back-pressure and stalls.
- Putting the pump after the filter keeps the whole line flooded and lets gravity do part of the work.

Powering the Waterfall

The waterfall was attached to the skimmer and designed as a summer-only system. Have you ever put your fingers into a running stream in winter? The water is often colder than the air.

Water loses heat quickly and warms slowly. Moving water cools even faster because of convective heat transfer, which makes it feel colder than still water—especially on your skin. If your pond has salt in it, the freezing point depression effect lowers the freezing point slightly (to around 28.4°F (-2°C) at typical koi-pond levels), so it can stay liquid a bit below the freezing point. But it isn't actually "colder than freezing"—it just resists freezing for a little longer.

This is why waterfalls should not run in winter—they chill the pond water faster, sometimes even below freezing. This is deadly to koi, who have nowhere to hide.

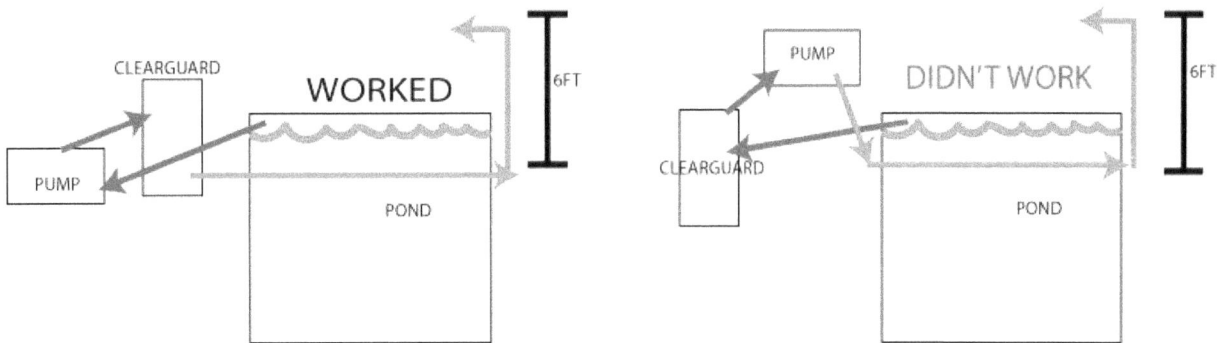

106 - *Pump configuration for waterfall*

In lakes, the depth protects fish using something called a thermocline. The surface water gets cold from the air, but the denser water below about 6–10 feet stays close to 39°F (4°C) . This happens because water is heaviest at that temperature, so it settles to the bottom and stays insulated while the colder, lighter water floats on top. That stable bottom layer keeps fish safe during winter—and 39°F (4 °C) is about as cold as koi should ever have to experience.

Knowing this, we installed an external pump in the shed and pushed the water to the waterfall. The problem was priming the pump.

We used a submersible pump and shoved its outlet pipe into the skimmer port that led to the shed. The pump itself was in the pond. Jim was lightly holding onto the pump so it didn't drop to the bottom (remember—no stairs).

When I plugged in the pump, there was a great surge of water and the hose came flying out of the skimmer, doing the can-can in the air and soaking everything and everyone. 2,000 gph is a lot of water.

Okay—try again. This time, Jim held the pipe inside the skimmer. Jim wrestled the hose like an Amazonian water snake while I waited at the shed pump, hand on the pipe. As soon as I felt vibrations in that pump, I knew the water had flooded it and I could turn it on.

A few minutes later—and yes, it took nearly three minutes—water spilled from the waterfall. It was a sight to behold.

The pump stays primed even during power failures. The only time we have to do this little dance again is when we remove the pump. Later, when we switched to a submersible pump, there was no issue at all.

We eventually added a second ClearGuard to the skimmer-waterfall system. We thought we would have to plumb it the same way as the deep water return, so Joe came back and moved all the pipes around. He fought with the pump system for an entire weekend to get it to pull the water through the filter and push it to the waterfall, but it would never hold prime.

It was a very puzzling problem. No matter what he did, the pump would lose suction. So, we pushed the water through the filter like normal—and it worked perfectly.

Why that configuration worked while the deep water return needed a different setup is still a mystery. Joe, a perfectionist, hated not knowing. But it's still working as it should today.

The Science: What Happened on the Waterfall Line

What happened when pump was between filter and waterfall
(ClearGuard → Pump → 2 ft down → 25 ft → 6 ft up to waterfall)
- The line dipped down before rising to the waterfall, creating a low point where air could collect.
- After shutdown, water drained back and air filled the high uphill section.

When you restarted:
- The pump was now pulling water through the filter (suction side)
- But it had to pull it uphill, through air trapped in that low point
- Centrifugal pumps can't pull air, so they just spun → cavitation → no prime

Result: The pump never got water to its impeller → no suction, no flow.

Configuration that worked:
Pump → ClearGuard → 2 ft down → 25 ft → 6 ft up to waterfall
- The pump sits below the pond water level → always flooded suction.
- When the pump starts, it's already full of water—and can push immediately.
- Even if there's air in the pipe, the pump pushes water behind it, and the air gets carried out the top at the waterfall.
- Once full, the line stays primed unless drained.

Result: Air is expelled naturally → the pump stays flooded → reliable prime every time.

The Key Principle
- When the pump is before the filter and below the pond water level, it's always primed.
- That's why it can safely push the air out.

- When it was after the filter, it wasn't flooded anymore and couldn't pull through the air pocket → instant failure.

Filtering the Filter

We have one of the best rotary drum filters on the market—the ProfiDrum. An RDF separates solids from the water before the water goes to a biofilter. This makes the biofilter far more efficient. The solids are washed out, and the manufacturer even recommends putting that output "tea" on your garden—it's full of nutrients plants love.

There's only one problem with that in Canada: winter.

The first winter, the tea froze—in the pipe. That caused an unpleasant mess. We thought of draining the tea into a Rubbermaid tote and using a sump pump, but in -40°F (-40°C) it just froze again.

My husband came up with a hilarious solution. He filters the 'tea' through a kitchen sieve perched over a bucket, then empties the solids every few hours. The waste water travels down a long pipe to the back of the property where it gets absorbed into the ground. It doesn't freeze quite as fast because he wrapped the pipe with heating cable designed for rain gutters (eavestroughing).

I suspect because the ProfiDrum was designed in Germany, they didn't have a solution for -40°F (-40°C) removal.

Cladding the Styrofoam

107 - *Early 2022 - Stone cladding nearly finished*

got it finished during the summer.

We knew we wanted to clad the ICF walls with stone to give it a sleek modern look. We chose "faux" stone cladding—light, easy to work with, and supposedly suitable for exterior use.

Our helper started by attaching a level ledger board across the bottom of the walls, which would eventually be covered by the finished grade of the patio. Between COVID-19 shutdowns, he got most of one wall done, but couldn't finish. Jim took over, learning as he went.

This was another learning curve for us—tiling was similar, but this was a cross between bricklaying and tiling. Jim did a wonderful job and

135

What we didn't know was that it needed to be waterproofed and resealed every year. After just one winter, there were patches crumbling apart. Even after I sealed the stone with the product the company recommended, it didn't stop the winter damage.

When we eventually have to replace that product, I think I'll go for ceramic tiles instead.

Capping the Walls

The walls ended up about 5–6" (~15cm) higher than planned. They were supposed to be comfortable sitting height—about 18" (~46cm)—but at 24–26" (~65cm) they were just a bit too tall to perch on.

I had originally planned to use capstones, but they were too short to cover the width of the wall, and the few large enough were far outside our budget.

So we used our patio slabs across the top to anchor the liner in place, cemented them down, and cut them to go around the TojaGrid posts. Once finished, if you squinted a bit, it looked almost professional.

It's not perfect, but it works—and that counts for a lot.

Shading the Pond

Shade is vital for keeping algae under control.

We were lucky: the Maple Tree we planted shortly after moving in was now a towering 40-foot (12.2m) giant that shaded our entire patio—and the pond—from about 2:00 on.

We also installed shades on the TojaGrid structure. They catch leaves, seeds, and bird droppings, and from above they make it harder for birds of prey to spot the fish.

108 - *Shading with TojaGrid*

New Fish and a Peaceful Pond

In late 2022, friends of ours had to sell their property—and they didn't want their koi to fall into careless hands. Luckily, our 9,500-gallon (~35,000 litres) pond was large enough to hold their thirteen fish alongside our six. We set up a quarantine tank to check them out before adding them.

Their old pond was barely 2,000 (~7,500 litres) gallons. Their three-year-olds looked like six-month-olds. They simply had no room to grow.

You should have seen those fish as they were put into our tank. At first they were confused. They didn't recognize where they were. They were used to being transported, as their owners brought them inside every winter, but this place was dark and strange. Where was the bottom?

One of our fish greeted them as each one arrived. Another of our school took them down to the others huddling at the bottom. You could see when they recognized a familiar face—the whole group would swim up to greet them and then go back down together.

The Science: Why Faux Stone Fails in Freeze-Thaw

Faux stone cladding is lightweight and easy to use, but often porous. Moisture seeps in, and when temperatures drop, it freezes and expands—a process called freeze–thaw weathering.

Each freeze–thaw cycle widens tiny cracks, flaking and crumbling the surface. Even sealing can't fully stop water from sneaking into unsealed edges or hairline gaps.

If you want a truly permanent finish in cold climates, use frost-proof materials like porcelain or ceramic tiles—they're dense, non-porous, and shrug off winter.

The Science: Why Waterfalls Shouldn't Run in Winter

Moving water loses heat fast through convective heat transfer. In winter, a running waterfall mixes cold surface water into the warmer bottom water, stripping away the pond's natural thermal layering.

In cold weather, ponds form a thermocline: dense water at 39°F (4°C) sinks to the bottom while near-freezing water floats above. Koi rely on this stable warm layer to survive.

Running the waterfall destroys this refuge, cooling the entire pond and risking temperatures too low for koi to survive. Shutting it down lets the warm bottom layer stay intact and protects your fish all winter.

The Science: Why Bigger Ponds Make Bigger Fish

Genetics plays a big role in how big your Koi will get. The "best" koi in the world grow to be behemoths. All you need to do is look for koi breeders on YouTube to see that.

It's no secret that a small pond will not grow big fish. It will limit their growth. But this is why they grow bigger in a large pond.

Larger ponds dilute fish waste, so ammonia and nitrate stay lower, reducing stress and boosting immune systems. (Remember me saying the larger the body of water, the easier it is to maintain?)

More swimming space builds muscle, while stable water volume buffers against temperature swings and pH crashes. This all fuels steady growth and vitality.

Space and water quality give koi the chance to thrive—and size is their thank-you.

Depth and length build their conformation into peak efficiency.

The Science: Why Shade Helps Fish and Water Quality

Sunlight powers photosynthesis, which fuels algae blooms. Shade reduces light penetration, limiting algae growth and keeping the water clearer.

Shade also prevents thermal stratification spikes in shallow water. On sunny days, shallow ponds can heat up rapidly at the surface, stressing fish and lowering dissolved oxygen levels.

Overhead shade cloths, pergolas, or trees keep temperatures steadier, reduce stress, and—as a bonus—block aerial predators from spotting your fish.

Where We Are Now?

It has taken seven long years to reach this point in 2025. There were times we nearly gave up, times we couldn't imagine living any other kind of life. Our friends have always thought us eccentric for pouring so much into this "hobby," and some of our family still don't understand it. But those of you who dream of a pond—of koi gliding just outside your door—know that it's not a hobby at all. It's a lifelong devotion.

Our fish finally escaped their basement prison in the spring of 2022. For the first time, they entered a real pond, one with a sophisticated filter system, room to grow and—most importantly—room to swim. At last, they were home.

Today, mid-September 2025, the pond is sheltered once again under a koi dome, this time supported by a sturdy Toja Grid system. Over the past three years Jim and I have perfected the installation so we can put it up in less than a day, and take it down just as quickly.

109 - *Shade (Soragoi) and Toronto (Bekko) eating watermelon*

Still, we're always looking for ways to make life easier. As the years pass, some jobs feel heavier, so I've set my sights on a "net-zero" maintenance pond. We now keep spare pumps ready so failures can be swapped instantly. The Zakki filter runs without fuss, though its ceramic media will need to be replaced gradually over the years. The ProfiDrum mostly looks after itself, though we still keep a watchful eye on the mechanics. Our two ClearGuard filters are brilliant because every single part—down to the O-rings—can be replaced. One of ours even cracked, and we were able to repair it instead of replace it. Their built-in UV lights can be changed as needed. Everything in the filter shed was chosen because it is low-maintenance, durable, and fixable.

That doesn't stop Jim, of course. Every day—two or three times a day—he makes his rounds. He doesn't need to, but he enjoys it: checking the pumps, the filters, the backup systems, manually flushing solids from the ProfiDrum, switching the aerators. It's his ritual, his way of staying close to the pond.

The fish themselves have thrived. After three years in their 9,500-gallon home, Caesar, Miss Piggy, Shade, Toronto, Bruce, and Goldie have grown to over 36 inches long—truly enormous koi. The younger ones are catching up fast. Last year we added an automatic feeder, but they still expect their daily treat: a quarter wedge of watermelon. Shade, especially, goes wild for it. We also spoil them with the occasional feast of thawed shrimp—whole now, because they no longer need me to cut them into bite-sized pieces.

110 - *2025, New patio, new Gazebo, and a working pond*

In spite of life's interruptions, we spend as much time with the fish as we can. And I am glad—truly glad—we chose this path.

Are we finished? Not quite. There's always something to improve, some way to make the pond even more effortless. I'd say we're about 90% of the way to that dream of low-maintenance bliss. For now, we can sit by the water, watch the koi glide, and reflect on how far we've come.

Do I regret it? Not really.

But if I began again, I would begin with clearer eyes—knowing the cost, and knowing the gift.

There is always something to improve, that's the nature of keeping fish.

Now… how am I going to build that staircase?

This year, 2025, we finally got the patio relaid, the gazebo for us built, and a deck made at the house. The cats have their catio and tunnels to run through, we have our space, and the Koi are right there too.

111 - *Another year, and ready for winter.*

You can see the greenhouse cover is on early. That is to maintain the water temperature as the season shuts down. It's late summer at the time of this writing, and the water is still 72°F (22°C).

Afterword

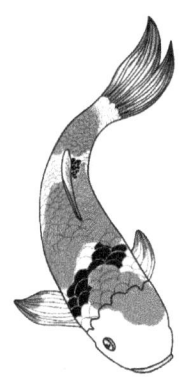

Koi are social fish. They are intelligent, have good eyesight, see in full color, hear well, and live a long time. Because of that, I believe they also have excellent memory. They demonstrate compassion and empathy, and they are tough fish.

The Japanese revere these fish. The Koi represents luck, prosperity, perseverance, strength, and transformation. I can certainly attest to this—we've had to be all of these. It requires perseverance especially to keep them; you need to be strong of will, and have the ability to constantly learn

Our fish have survived and thrived in spite of our many mistakes. Each mistake taught us something, and each fish showed us their grit, their fight for life, and their sense of humor.

Yes—humor. One of our koi, Shade, loves watermelon. She'll get under the shell and boost it up out of the water, swimming around with it on her head like a hat.

Caesar, the female we had for many years, was known for moving pots of water lilies. One day they'd be in a different corner. Or floating on the surface.

Another of our fish, Zoom, loved racing across the surface like a shark making waves with his dorsal fin. These fish have personality, and many will eat out of your hand.

Whatever the reason you end up keeping koi, you'll learn from them as well as about them. They make wonderful additions to your family. They like people, and will swim with you. They recognize your voice and will come 'running' over to greet you when they hear your approach.

Most of all, their environment is soothing to the human soul and spirit.

I hope you've enjoyed our story—laughed at what we did wrong, and learned from what we did right.

Now, when I sit by the water and listen to the soft hum of the pumps, I remember every disaster, every victory—and smile. In the end this was a DIY of sorts. It's all possible.

And finally...*everything works.*

113 - Winter 2024/2025

Appendix A – Pipe Sizes & Flow Rates

For PVC pipe and flex PVC pipe—Schedule 40

Pipe Size	Inside Diameter	Typical Flow (GPH)	Notes
1 ½"	1.61"	~3.500	Small ponds, short runs only
2"	2.07"	~4,800-5000 GPH	Standard for most ponds
3"	3.07"	~9,000 GPH	Good for gravity fed RDFs
4"	4.03"	~13,000 GPH	Bottom drains and main lines

Note: Larger pipes reduce friction loss and improve efficiency.

Appendix B – Pipe Types

Pipe Type	Strength	Pressure Rating	Best Use	Notes
ABS	Lightweight, brittle, black	Not pressure-rated	Gravity-fed lines	Easy to cut/glue; cheaper, but not for pumps.
PVC (Sched 20)	Thin-walled, white	Light duty	Central Vacuums	Not for water use
PVC (Sched 40)	Strong, thick, white	Pressure-rated 120-160 PSI	Pump lines, buried pipe	Gold standard for ponds
PVC (Sched 80)	Extra thick, grey	Heavy duty 200-280 PSI	Industrial	Overkill for ponds.
PVC Conduit	Flexible, grey	No	Electrical, running wires	Not for Water
Flex PVC 2" or 4"	Black or White, Strong	Pressure rated ~100 PSI	Long runs – allows for curves without elbows	Not good for tight spaces Not UV resistant

Appendix C – Valve Types

Type	Use	Pros	Cons	Notes
Ball Valve	On/off flow control	Cheap, reliable, simple	Hard to adjust flow precisely	Use full-port so the inside opening matches the pipe size
Gate Valve	Fine flow control	Very precise adjustment	Large, bulky, more expensive	Great for gravity-fed systems
Check Valve	Stops backflow	Keeps pumps primed	Can stick open or closed	Install vertically or on horizontal runs with swing type
Union Ball Valve	Isolation & disconnection	Easy equipment removal	Slightly larger & pricier	Best before and after pumps, filters, UVs
Swing Check Valve	Stops reverse siphon	Silent, low resistance	Needs horizontal run	Perfect after external pumps
Spring Check Valve	Stops backflow in any position	Works vertical or horizontal	Adds resistance and can clog	Only use on clean water lines

For PVC Pipe and Flex PVC systems

PRO TIP: *Always place valves and unions before and after major equipment (pumps, filters, UV, heaters) so you can remove them easily. Use true-union ball valves wherever possible—they last longer and make servicing painless. Avoid too many valves: every one adds friction loss.*

Appendix D – Glue vs Cement

First of all, you don't glue PVC pipe together. You weld it with a two step process. It's called PVC Cement.

What's the Difference?

PVC cement doesn't just stick pieces together—it chemically melts the surfaces and fuses them into one solid piece.
PVC glue (like wood or craft glue) is not for pressure plumbing and will fail under water pressure.
So when working with PVC pipe or flex PVC pipe for pond plumbing, always use PVC cement—never ordinary glue.

Primer + Cement: The Right Method

*   Use PVC primer (purple or clear) first—it softens and cleans the surface.
*   Apply a generous, even coat of PVC cement to both the pipe and the fitting.
*   Push the pipe fully into the fitting and twist ¼ turn to spread the cement evenly.
*   Hold for 30 seconds while it sets (especially on large pipe).
*   Let joints cure at least 24 hours before pressure-testing.
NOTE   For flex PVC, use medium- or heavy-bodied PVC cement (often labeled "for flexible PVC") so it bonds through the soft wall fully.

Common Mistakes
*   Skipping primer → weak, leaky joints
*   Using glue instead of cement → joint failure under pressure
*   Not pushing pipe in fully → dry spots → leaks
*   Moving the joint before it sets → breaks the seal

Appendix E – Weatherproofing

Protecting your pipes from frost, floods, and storms

Frost Protection

- In cold climates, bury your PVC pipe or flex PVC pipe below the local frost line (depth where soil freezes solid).
- Frost line varies:
- ~12" (30 cm) in mild zones
- 36–48" (90–120 cm) or more in cold northern zones
- Pipes must slope to drain if they'll be emptied seasonally.
- Where burying isn't possible, insulate pipes with foam wrap and use pipe heating cable.

NOTE   Frost heave can shear fittings right off. Keep all buried plumbing below freeze depth and on undisturbed soil.

Flood Resilience

- Place pumps, electrical, and filters above known flood level (or on raised platforms).
- Install check valve on return lines to prevent reverse siphon when water rises.
- Anchor filter housings and pipes to resist floating or shifting.
- If you're in a high water table area, weigh down buried pipes with sand backfill or strapping.

NOTE   Flood water is full of silt—design your pond to keep it out of the pond system, not just off your lawn.

Storm & Wind Protection

- Use flexible couplings near equipment to absorb vibration and ground movement.
- Anchor exposed pipes, pumps, and filters so high winds can't shift or topple them.
- If hurricanes or severe windstorms are possible:
- Secure covers and domes
- Drain or lower water level slightly to allow for heavy rainfall
- Disconnect and cap above-ground plumbing if debris impact is likely

NOTE   In extreme events, protect the infrastructure first—fish can survive without pumps for a while, but pumps won't survive flying tree branches.

For More Information Online on Frost Line Reference Links

List of Photographs

List of Science Tips

Index

www.ingramcontent.com/pod-product-compliance
Lightning Source LLC
Chambersburg PA
CBHW041140120626
46547CB00020B/3059